Baseball by the Numbers

Baseball by the
NUMBERS

*How Statistics Are Collected,
What They Mean, and
How They Reveal the Game*

by WILLIE RUNQUIST

McFarland & Company, Inc., Publishers
Jefferson, North Carolina, and London

British Library Cataloguing-in-Publication data are available

Library of Congress Cataloguing-in-Publication Data

Runquist, Willie, 1930–
    Baseball by the numbers : how statistics are collected, what
they mean, and how they reveal the game / by Willie
Runquist.
        p. cm.
    Includes index.
    ISBN 0-7864-0006-4 (sewn softcover : 50# alk. paper)
    1. Baseball—Statistical methods. I. Title.
GV877.R86 1995
796.357′021—dc20   94-8901
                                                                         CIP

Manufactured in the United States of America

McFarland & Company, Inc., Publishers
  Box 611, Jefferson, North Carolina 28640

Contents

Preface

Baseball is a game that can be enjoyed at many levels. If you do not enjoy baseball's numbers or are of that radical fringe that thinks that numbers somehow ruin the game, this book is not for you. I make no apologies, nor am I trying to convert anyone. As far as I am concerned, baseball statistics are amoral. They are neither good nor bad, they simply are. And for me they are fun. They can, if used properly, provide insight into this wonderfully complex and profound game. If you are inclined to explore the numbers, welcome aboard. If you are only concerned with baseball's charm and ambience, the private lives and psyches of its players, or want to quaff a cold one and root-root-root for the home team, I have no quarrel. I like those things about baseball too, but this book is about its numbers.

I have tried to write for the statistically knowledgeable but nonpracticing fan. This is not a book *of* statistics but a book *about* statistics. You will find no new and astounding lists of the ten greatest players of all time, no ranking of last year's second basemen in their ability to turn the double play, no compilation of lefty-righty stats, no snappy new statistic claimed to be the final, ultimate, everlasting, never-to-be-exceeded perfect measure of performance. In fact, there is really very little here that is new. But I hope you will find some insight into how baseball collects its numbers, what they mean, and how they can be and are manipulated to understand more about the game and its players.

Neophytes will definitely benefit from reading this book, particularly the first six chapters and Chapter 12. The other chapters may be tough sledding even for the statistically knowledgeable. This is not a "sit by the fire and browse" kind of book. Unless you have some feel for baseball numbers, statistical reasoning, or both, it may take a bit of effort. But as they say, "No pain, no gain!" It might be advisable to go slowly and consume a little bit at a time to avoid indigestion.

I have tried to make the presentation intuitive rather than technical, and as much as possible to avoid the jargon of the professional statistician. At the same time, it is necessary not to compromise the concepts. There are no proofs to be found, however, and much will have to be taken on faith. After all, we are concerned with data analysis, not formal statistics.

Baseball statisticians are a notoriously enthusiastic lot. (Who else could

1

get excited about *secondary average?*) Enthusiasm is admirable, but after all, statistics are nothing more than the result of arithmetic performed on numbers, and the conclusions one may legitimately draw depend upon two things: (1) what the numbers represent; (2) what the arithmetic did to them. I have tried to look at baseball's statistics for what the numbers can and cannot tell us based on the source of the numbers (the data if you will) and the arithmetic.

Nevertheless, the book is not an annotated compendium of traditional and *Sabermetric* statistics. It is not intended to be historically or contemporaneously complete. The focus is on the statistical rather than the logical or theoretical properties of measures, and it is not intended to be exhaustively critical. With the exception of some traditional measures, a particular statistic is introduced to exemplify a general point about its structure, not to criticize or praise it as a measure of some particular quality.

I have included detailed calculations for many analyses. At the risk of getting the reader mired down in the arithmetic, I did this for two reasons. First, it is often difficult to understand a procedure unless you can see firsthand what is happening to the numbers. Second, there is always the possibility that someone will wish to carry out some calculations on particular data. Readers may wish to skip over the more elaborate calculations at first reading, particularly those in Chapter 14. They are not as forbidding as they appear, however. Most of the procedures can be carried out quite efficiently on small data bases with nothing more than a desktop calculator, or on larger data bases with a home computer.

I spent 40 years of my life as a research psychologist. A good part of my training and vocational activity was in the statistical analysis of behavioral data. It seems to me that baseball numbers are nothing if not behavioral data, and statistical procedures that have proved valuable in social science research are admirably suited to deal with the kinds of problems that baseball generates. I am not, however, a statistician by trade, so my approach is to apply well-established and time-proven analytic procedures rather than indulge in creative statistical innovation.

My goal is to provide a better understanding of what traditional statistics really are and to make the reader a more informed consumer of statistical innovations. Baseball analysis, however, has become a highly technical and creative area of applied statistics, and this book makes no pretense of being on the cutting edge of this innovation. With some exceptions (especially Chapter 17), I have dealt with the traditional data base that is easily available to the public in newspapers and baseball guides.

Despite all of these disclaimers, not all the procedures described are in common use by baseball analysts, particularly those discussed in chapters 7, 8, 13, and 14. It is my studied opinion that they should be. Questions regarding the reliability of differences between players, differences due to playing conditions, and the accuracy of prediction formulae have not always been properly addressed even though well-established procedures are available to do so. I have carried out just enough of these analyses to know that we have accepted far too many facts as general truths without proper statistical support. Some of those procedures are presented in the hope that they will become more commonplace. Yet I have not exhausted the file of possible analytic procedures. The next step would be the application of procedures known to social scientists as *multivariate analyses*. I have only barely scratched the surface of these procedures, the understanding of which almost requires formal training and special mathematical skills.

I have my own opinions regarding the usefulness of certain measures and I have my own favorite statistics, but I have tried to keep my focus on statistical rather than substantive issues, or at worst present both sides of a controversial situation. If my biases occasionally sneak in, so be it. This is neither the time nor place for polemics, and I do not wish to encourage debate about matters of taste or theoretical preference in these pages. If you choose to believe in clutch hitters and are in love with secondary average and *range factors*, you may do so without eliciting disparagement from me.

It is customary for the author to conclude his self-immolation by briefly crediting those that have helped him unburden his mind and soul. My wife, Peggy, who taught behavioral statistics at the University of Alberta for ten years, was my reluctant sounding board. She has, I believe, grown from a mild tolerance to a complete disinterest in baseball statistics as the result of my incessant interruptions of her daily activities with yet another statistical conundrum. Nevertheless, she was ever ready to correct my assumptions when I got carried away and to prevent me from opening can after can of statistical worms. She certainly wonders at times what kind of weirdo she married.

Perhaps my biggest debt is to my academic colleagues and students whose brains I picked while learning and practicing my trade. The most incisive colleagues were Stan Rule, Geoff Keppel, Bill Rozeboom, and Graham Bell. I doubt if they realized where their expertise would lead me since they scarcely know the difference between a home run and an infield fly. Yet, I cannot saddle them with the blame for any of my peccadilloes.

I also owe a real debt to three publications. John Thorne and Pete Palmer's *The Hidden Game of Baseball* and *Total Baseball* provided a secondary access to the minds of Sabermetricians. The boys and girls at Stats, Inc., publishers of *The Baseball Scoreboard,* managed to provide glimpses of their incredible data base and continue to ask the kind of interesting questions to which traditional inferential statistics could be applied. I do not always agree with their conclusions, but the value of their work is immense.

Willie Runquist
Union Bay, B.C.
Canada

Prologue: In the Beginning Were the Numbers

Statistics are not about baseball but about the numerical records of baseball. Not records like "the most broken-bat singles by one-eyed left-handed third basemen during a war year" but records as numerical information about games that have been played. Statistical analysis consists of performing simple arithmetic on those records. If you can add, subtract, multiply, and divide (along with finding the occasional square root), you can do statistics.

Some philosopher, immortalized in the movie *Bull Durham,* once said, "Baseball is a very simple game; you throw the ball, you hit the ball, you catch the ball." Statistically, baseball is a very simple game. Players come to bat one at a time and either make an out or reach base. If they reach base, they either advance to score a run, make an out on the bases, or are left on base. When the batters on each team have recorded 27 (or so) outs, we end the game and declare the team that has the larger number of runs the winner. The records or data of the game consist of the number of times various things happened during the game and sometimes the sequence in which they occurred.

Baseball statistics serve two distinctly different purposes. One is to evaluate the performance of individual players. Baseball statisticians are quite fond of compiling lists of the 10 or 20 "best" players based on one statistic or another. While these lists may be interesting in their own right, they can serve the more serious purpose of telling us how a player is likely to perform in the future or in the case of professional baseball players, his place in the list may determine his salary or whether he keeps his job.

The second purpose of statistics is to provide some understanding of how the events of a game influence the outcome of that game. Suppose we have a runner on first base and no one out in the fifth inning with a one-run lead. What is likely to happen if we sacrifice or attempt a stolen base at this point? There are also general questions, such as whether differences exist between play on natural grass and artificial turf or whether a group of players performs differently when batting against left- and right-handed pitchers.

Apart from these purposes, statistics have two important functions.

Descriptive statistics are used simply to describe or summarize a set of numbers. The result applies only to those numbers and hence represents a "fact." When one says that Don Mattingly had a batting average of .303 in 1989, the batting average is being used as a descriptive statistic. It tells us something about Mattingly's performance in 1989 and implies nothing more.

Statistics may also be used to make *inferences* about other events. In this case, a statistic is considered to be representative of more than just the observations on which it is computed. Does Mattingly's batting average mean that we can expect him to have a similar average next year? Or we observe that 15 players had a better overall batting average in home games than road games in 1990. Does this mean that batting averages are generally better at home than on the road, or does the result apply just to those 15 players for those particular games for that year? Statistical procedures may help answer such questions.

Categorizing the Outcomes

The number of things that are possible each time a batter faces a pitcher is enormous, and baseball is interesting as a spectator sport because no two happenings are ever exactly alike. To count the things that happen during games, record keepers have developed a limited number of categories into which each event is placed. In the final analysis, these categories determine what we can learn about the game from its records. When something happens to create an out, enable the batter to reach base, or advance a runner from one base to another, something is recorded. A lot of things are usually not recorded. We do not record the number of times the pitcher adjusts his clothing or scratches himself, or the number of times a batter spits. More seriously, the individual balls and strikes thrown to a batter or the foul balls he hits have not been recorded. Neither have the pitcher's throws to first base to hold a runner on base. Sometimes there are special records of these events, particularly in recent seasons, but they are not part of the official record.

The most important thing about a category is that once an event is placed in a category, it is treated the same as every other event in that category. For example, one of the categories is home runs. A home run usually occurs when a fair ball clears the outfield fence. Whether the batter put the ball in orbit or barely cleared the wall with a windblown pop fly does not matter. It is simply recorded as a home run. Likewise, a single could be a line smash through the middle, a pop fly that fell between the fielders, a ball hit too slowly to be fielded in time, a perfectly placed bunt, a ground ball that took a bad bounce, etc. A single is a single is a single, and as the immortal bard of baseball once said, "They all look like line drives the next morning." No statistical procedure, no matter how complex or sophisticated, can separate the events combined in a category.

The definitions of the categories used for the *official* records are contained in the scoring rules that are part of the official rules of baseball. Like the rules and customs of the game, the scoring rules have changed over the years, with the result that the categories, and hence the data, are not always the same from year to year. While the names of the categories are relatively self-explanatory (singles, doubles, runs batted in, runs scored, etc.), they are usually abbreviated in summaries that report the data, and occasionally in discussions (e.g., RBIs, or "ribbies"). For those who are not familiar with the system, a glossary of abbreviations is presented in Appendix A.

How Events Are Counted

The procedure for assigning an event to a category is just as important as the definition of the categories. In professional baseball, the official scorer has the sole authority to assign the result of every player's appearance at the plate to the appropriate category or categories. On occasion, a decision must also be made about how a runner advances (stolen base, passed ball, wild pitch, etc.). In practice, many decisions are not simple, and while the scoring rules give guidance to the scorer, the final decision depends solely on his judgment.

Whenever human judgment is involved, there is a question of the *reliability* of the judgments. Reliability has nothing to do with accuracy but simply means consistency—consistency for a given scorer from inning to inning and day to day, and consistency among different scorers in different places and different times. Consistency means that whatever the time, place, or circumstance, or who is making the judgment, the category a given event is assigned to is the same. It should not depend upon who is scoring a play or when it is scored.

How good is the reliability of scorers? First, it depends on the categories involved. Many scoring decisions are relatively unambiguous if one follows the guidance provided by the rule book (e.g., base on balls, run batted in), but a few are quite difficult, and much is left to the discretion of the scorer. The touchiest one is undoubtedly the distinction between a hit and an error. Although there are several other categories where judgment is equally difficult, the identification of success with hits and failure with errors ensures the emotional involvement of players and fans in the decision and puts considerable pressure on the scorer. There are seven criteria listed in the scoring rules to tell the scorer when a hit should and should not be credited. Somewhat paraphrased, these are:

A batter *is* credited with a hit if he reaches base when
1. A ball hits the fence or ground without being touched by a fielder.
2. A ball is hit so hard or slowly that the fielder cannot make a play. (Even if he interferes with a player who could have made the play.)
3. A batted ball takes a bad hop and cannot be handled with ordinary effort by the fielder.
4. A ball is hit untouched to the outfield and cannot be handled with ordinary effort.
5. A batted ball hits a runner or the umpire (except infield flies).
6. A fielder's choice fails, and the batter would not have been put out.
7. An exceptional play fails to get him out. (The batter gets the benefit of the doubt.)

He is *not* credited with a hit when there is
1. A force out or botched force out.
2. He hits safely, but the runner fails to touch the next base.
3. A runner is out on a fielder's choice (nonforce), or there is a botched fielder's choice.
4. A late fielder's choice if the batter would have been out.
5. A runner-batter's interference, unless the batter would have been safe.

As complicated as this may seem, the difficulty resides in just two decisions: What constitutes "ordinary effort"? Would the batter have reached first base safely regardless of what else happened on the play? Such judgments require that the scorer understand the difficulty of various plays and the ability of the fielder, and he must be better than the umpire at making "safe-out" decisions since that judgment often has to be made without the play actually taking place.

The fact of the matter is that we probably do not know how reliable the scorers are or have been in crediting a hit. No one appears to have checked on this. Whether the batter, the fielder, 90 percent of the fans, or members of the media agree with a decision is not particularly relevant. The scorer is the one that makes the decision, and it is *consistency* by and between scorers that is at issue. This is not to say that one could not make scoring decisions in some other manner. For example, a scoring committee could vote on every questionable play after examining 10 television replays from different angles (this may be occurring informally in some cases). Or we could let the batter decide—a procedure that would no doubt result in more hits and fewer errors.

But in the end the decision must be a judgment, and the best that can be hoped for is that all scorers apply the same criteria. Scorers, however, are human, and there has been enough research on human judgment to indicate that all may not be well. For example, there is considerable pressure on scorers to change their criteria when a no-hitter or a consecutive-game hitting streak is on the line. The fielder's or batter's reputation may also bias scoring decisions.

Do not confuse this issue with the question of whether the scorer made the *correct* decision. There is no right or wrong decision because there is no objective way to determine the true category a result should be assigned to. In matters of judgment, the scorer is correct, by definition. But lack of consistency or reliability does have an effect on the quality of the data available for statistical analysis. In other words, if some of the hits obtained by a batter would have been scored as errors by another scorer or would have been scored as errors if hit by another batter, the numbers we work with do not truly represent what happened.

There is one consolation, however. Unlike the decisions of umpires, inconsistency in scoring decisions has no effect on winning and losing games, only on the record of the game and its performers. Thus, any problem with the reliability of scorers may prove vexatious to statisticians, players, and others who make serious use of the statistics, but to those who are concerned only with the score of the game, it matters not.

Producing Totals and Summaries

The exact sequence of events in a game is also recorded by the official scorer, although the exact sequence of events has generally not been retained. The permanent record of a game is usually a summary report of the frequency of events in each category for each batter, pitcher, and fielder, which is sent to the league office. Not only the scoring rules but also the structure of the official summary have been changed every so often, so that a given category may not mean the same thing from year to year.

One form of game summary may be published in newspapers as the familiar *box score*. Box scores vary considerably and usually do not contain all the categories provided in official league summaries. The information reported in box scores has also changed over the years, and some of the official scoring categories have seldom been included (e.g., caught stealing). Newspaper box scores also differ from the official record of a game and may contain errors but often are the only data available since most leagues, even at the professional level, have not retained the official summaries.

The data from box scores or official summaries for several games may be combined to produce more extensive sets of data, and it is usually these combined summaries that provide the numbers for statistical analysis. Seasonal summaries appearing in various baseball publications represent the combined frequencies in each category for all games played in a season, but summaries can also be made for any subset of games, such as games played on the home field, on artificial turf, indoors, against a particular team, or during a particular time span (month or week). With the advent of computerized records, summaries for these subsets of data are more readily available, although they are not part of the official records and except for recent years may not exist.

It is also possible to abstract sets of plate appearances for a particular player and treat those separately. Thus, we may have summaries of appearances with men in scoring position, leading off an inning, or terminating with various ball-strike counts. Like data for special subsets of games, these records are available only for recent years and are not part of the official records.

Other baseball data are not part of the game itself but refer to players' individual skills. Speed of pitches, base-running speed, and bat speed are some of these. This book will not deal with these kinds of data.

1

Batting, Pitching, and Fielding Lines

Most fans think of baseball statistics in terms of individual players. Players also talk about their numbers. This section is concerned with those numbers and what they mean. Since all statistics should have a purpose, the purpose of these statistical procedures is to describe and evaluate the differences between players.

A single baseball season can generate an enormous amount of data. The basic data in the *Official Baseball Guide* consist of frequencies in 17 batting categories for every player, 22 pitching categories for every pitcher, and 5 fielding categories for every player at each position he played (6 categories for catchers), and the equivalent for each of the teams. *The Baseball Encyclopedia* and *Total Baseball,* which contain the records of every major league player and team since the sun first came up, each have close to 1 million pieces of data. Data may be organized in different ways—by teams, by seasons, by positions played—but the basic data are those for an individual player in which the frequency of events in each category is listed for a single season. We shall call these listings the *batting line,* the *pitching line,* and the *fielding line.* A typical batting line, for Tony Gwynn of San Diego for 1988:

G	AB	R	H	2B	3B	HR	RBI	SH	SF	HP	BB	SO	SB	CS	GDP
133	521	64	163	22	5	7	70	4	2	0	51	40	26	11	11

The pitching line for Dave Stieb of Toronto in 1988 would look like this:

G	CS	C	F	W	L	Sh	Sv	IP	H	BF	R	ER	HR	SH	SF	HB	BB	SO	WP	BK
32	31	8	1	16	8	4	0	207.1	157	844	76	70	15	0	4	13	79	147	4	5

A fielding line for Mattingly, the Yankees first baseman, in 1988:

G   PO   A   E   DP
143 1250 99   9   131

These lines are the ones that appear in baseball guides and other summaries. The categories reported are of various types. Some categories represent the *exhaustive and mutually exclusive* outcomes of a single plate appearance. In other words, the result of every plate appearance must be tallied in one and only one of these categories.

Not all of these mutually exclusive categories are included in the official batting line. Some of the above categories represent combined outcomes, but the individual frequencies may often be obtained by subtraction.

Some of the categories are *independent* of one another: An event may be placed in one regardless of whether it is also placed in another category.

The Batting Line

The mutually exclusive batting categories are singles, doubles, triples, home runs, sacrifices, sacrifice flies, bases on balls, hit by pitcher, strikeouts, and hit into double plays. The result of every plate appearance by a batter must be placed in one of those categories* or by default falls into *other outs,* which includes not only outs made by a batter but the number of times he reached base on a force play, some other fielder's choice, or an error. *Other outs* is obtained by subtracting *hits, strikeouts,* and *hit into double plays* from *at-bats* (AB − [H + SO + DP]), but in many analyses strikeouts and hit into double plays are combined with other outs to form a single category. *Singles* is obtained by subtracting *doubles, triples,* and *home runs* from hits (H − [2B + 3B + HR]). Because the categories are exhaustive and mutually exclusive, the sum of the individual components is equal to the actual number of plate appearances.

There are four other categories in the batting line. *Runs scored* is an exhaustive and mutually exclusive outcome of each plate appearance but is independent of all the other categories. A batter either scores a run or does not, but a run may occur along with any of the other categories. *Times caught stealing* has the same status; it either does or does not occur on a given plate appearance but represents an independent category.

First base awarded on fielder (catcher) interference is the only outcome not included in the batting line. This outcome happens so infrequently that it has little effect on the data. For trivia fans, catcher's interference occurs about once in every 10,000 plate appearances.

The frequencies of *runs batted in* and *stolen bases* do not represent a categorization of plate appearances. Players may receive from 0 to 4 runs batted in on a given plate appearance and from 0 to 3 stolen bases. Runs batted in is independent of every other category. Stolen bases are independent of other categories, but each stolen base represents an exhaustive and exclusive outcome of an attempted steal in which the alternative is *caught stealing*.

The structure of Gwynn's batting line is as follows:

									Total			Other
PA	1B	2B	3B	HR	BB	HB	SH	SF	Outs	SO	DP	Outs
578	129	22	5	7	51	0	4	2	358	40	11	307

Scoring			*Steals*		
R	NR	RBI	Att	SB	CS
64	514	70	37	26	11

The first value is the total number of times that Gwynn came to the plate that year. The next 12 categories represent the 12 mutually exclusive categories into which each plate appearance is categorized. The next three categories are related to scoring. The first two represent an exhaustive categorization of runs scored and not scored on each plate appearance. Runs batted in, an independent category, is the sum of runs batted in on each plate appearance. The last three categories are total attempted steals, broken down into successes and failures.

The Pitching Line

In the pitching line, the first eight categories represent the result of game appearances rather than batters faced. All other frequencies in the pitching line are based on the result of each batter faced by the pitcher, and like the batting line are a mixture of exhaustive mutually exclusive categories, independent categories, and combined categories.

Game appearances consist of several independent categories, each of which forms two exhaustive and mutually exclusive categories. Games may be either started or relieved. Relief appearances are obtained by subtracting starts from total games pitched (G – GS). *Games started* may be completed or not completed. Usually only complete games appear in the pitching line. *Games relieved* may be finished or not. In this case, games finished is included in the pitching line, and games not finished is obtained by subtracting them from relief appearances.

Games played may also be classified into decisions and nondecisions, the former into *wins* and *losses*. Games relieved may be classified into *saves* and *no saves*. No saves is not *blown saves*. A blown save is a category based on save opportunities. Neither datum is included in the official pitching line, although they may appear in some statistical records. No saves simply represents all relief appearances in which no save is recorded, for whatever reason.

The remainder of the pitching line, except for *wild pitches* and *balks*, is the same as the batting line, except that the combinations are different. Wild pitches and balks are simply two independent events that have the same logical status as stolen bases. They may occur one to three times per plate appearance. In the case of pitching, *batters faced* is the equivalent of plate appearances. The outcome for each batter faced is categorized as a *home run, other hit, base on balls, hit batter, sacrifice, sacrifice fly,* or *strikeout*. Singles, doubles, and triples are not differentiated for pitchers in the *official* summary but may be available in special publications. The remaining plate appearances are *other outs*. These categories are exactly equivalent to those in the batting line. Each batter faced also results in a run scored or no run scored, and every run is *earned* or *unearned. Innings pitched* is a unique category and has little to do with real innings. A pitcher receives credit for one-third of an inning pitched every time an out occurs while he is in the game. It is tangentially related to batters faced, but unrelated to other categories.

A rewritten pitching line for Stieb would be as follows:

Starts					Relieved				Decisions					
G	GS	CG	IG		GR	GF	NF		Tot	W	L	S	ND	Sho
32	31	8	23		1	1	0		24	16	8	0	8	4

Plate Appearances										Scoring				Misc.		
BF	HR	OH	BB	HB	SH	SF	SO	Out	Tot		NR	R	ER	UR	IP	WP	BK
844	15	142	79	13	0	4	147	444	591		768	76	70	6	207	4	5

The first seven categories are based on total games pitched (Tot). Starts and relief appearances are subsets that are broken down into their components. The next five categories are based on decisions. The total of the five categories sums to games pitched (G). *Shutouts* (Sho) is an independent category, although it could be a subset of wins. The second part of the line, based on plate appearances, is similar to the batting line. The category *Other hits* (OH) consists of singles, doubles, and triples. Runs are broken down into *earned* (ER) and *unearned* (UR). It would be possible to subdivide batters faced according to $3 \times$ innings pitched (outs), scored (R), and left on base (the remainder).

The Fielding Line

For fielding lines, the frequencies are based on fielding chances rather than batter appearances. Since a fielding chance is defined as a *putout,* an *assist,* or an *error,* these three outcomes form a set of mutually exclusive and exhaustive categories of fielding chances. *Double plays* are independent of fielding chances. For Mattingly, we have

TC   PO   A   E   DP
1358 1250 99 9 131

Special Problems with Definitions

The Official At-Bat

The official at-bat (AB) is one of the most frequently used statistics. At-bats are a subset of plate appearances. The development of the at-bat was motivated by the desire to base statistics on only those plate appearances in which the batter determined the outcome. Therefore, if he was given a base on balls, hit by the pitcher, or ordered by the manager to bunt into an out to advance a runner, those events were not considered his doing and should not count in evaluating his performance. At present, sacrifice flies are also excluded in determining official at-bats.

In addition to the official at-bat, there is another statistic that may be called the official plate appearance. Technically, plate appearances should equal the total number of times a batter comes to the plate and finishes his turn. It has become common practice, however, to exclude sacrifice bunts from actual plate appearances when computing various statistics because they are manager-ordered intentional outs. Henceforth, this definition will be used. Sacrifice flies, however, remain part of these official plate appearances, presumably because they are under the batter's control.

The sacrifice fly has had a checkered history in record keeping. It was credited from 1908 to 1930 and in 1939 but was not separated from sacrifice hits. Therefore, when sacrifices are subtracted from plate appearances in those years, an unknown number of sacrifice flies are also being subtracted. Sacrifices were inflated from 1927 to 1930 by counting fly balls that advanced a runner. As logical as this seems in view of the definition of a sacrifice bunt, it has not been used in this way since that time. A bunt out is not just a sacrifice on a squeeze play but any time a runner advances. Perhaps fly balls should gain equal privilege. From 1940 to 1953, the sacrifice fly was counted as any other fly out, except for the fact that it provided a run batted in. Therefore, run-scoring fly balls cannot be eliminated from plate appearances for those years. The rules have been as they are now since 1954, with the categories separately reported.

The reason for all of this waffling is that the sacrifice bunt is almost always an intentional out. The intent of a sacrifice fly is not nearly as clear. A batter may be trying to hit safely but fails; hence the out is not intentional. Rule makers have obviously vacillated in their attitude toward run-scoring fly balls, but in a purely statistical sense the reason for eliminating events from the total of at-bats was to correct a batter's plate appearances for situations where the opportunity to achieve a safe hit was eliminated. It was not intended to reward him for driving in a run. One could just as well make a legitimate case for subtracting an at-bat for runs driven in on ground balls or even runs driven in on double plays. According to present scoring conventions, a player is deprived of a run batted in in the latter case. Statistically, the logic of some of these arbitrary scoring rules appears somewhat twisted, regardless of their humanitarian qualities.

Pitching Decisions

A number of categories cause difficulties for pitchers. Although wins and losses are team statistics, they made considerable sense before about 1950 when the main reason for removing a pitcher was his ineffectiveness. At present, only about 15 percent of pitchers' games are complete games, and starting pitchers seldom last more than six or seven innings, even if pitching well. Wins and losses for pitchers have become largely irrelevant. Since a pitcher's fate often resides in the hands of the reliever, some have even suggested that there be *unwarranted wins* and *undeserved losses* or that games started be considered *quality starts* and (presumably) *nonquality starts*. Definitions for these categories are largely arbitrary constructions by various analysts and are not included in official scoring rules.

Runs and Earned Runs

The assignment of runs and earned runs to pitchers also produces inequities. The scoring rule admits of little ambiguity, but neither runs nor earned runs are a realistic assessment of pitching performance. Both earned and unearned runs are charged against the pitcher that put those runners on base. The more often a pitcher is relieved in midinning, the greater is his dependency on the performance of the reliever. He may benefit because the relief pitcher is effective, but he may also suffer if the fireman is carrying gasoline instead of water. Likewise, a reliever who enters an inning with outs already registered benefits by not having to obtain three outs before any runners he has put on base are "removed" by the termination of the inning.

The definition of *earned run* more than occasionally fails to capture the reality of the pitching performance. Whenever an inning would have ended had an error not occurred, any runs scoring after that point are unearned. A pitcher may totally disintegrate and give up a basketful of legitimate runs but is not penalized. The logic is that a pitcher should not have to get more than three "outs" in an inning, but the logic may be questioned if the inning drags on and on as a result of subsequent inept performance.

There are also peculiarities in the definition of *inning pitched*. The pitcher gets dinged when a runner that he put on base scores but receives no credit when that runner is put out running the bases. Moreover, he does not receive credit for one-third of an inning when the runner reaches base on an error despite the fact that were it not for the fielding faux pas, it would have been an out.

Fielding Chances

The assignment of a putout or assist when an out is made is relatively unambiguous. The definition of a *fielding chance,* however, leaves something to be desired. In more than a few instances, errors may be assigned to players when there was no opportunity for a putout or assist. These occur when a misplay allows a runner to advance a base. In this sense, a true fielding chance (opportunity for error) occurs whenever a player touches a ball in play, not just when that play eventually results in an out.

2

Basic Statistical Measures

Four basic statistics are useful for the analysis of baseball data: *proportion, mean, standard deviation,* and *correlation coefficient.*

Proportions

Proportions are formed by sorting things into exhaustive and mutually exclusive categories. The proportion of objects in a category is then defined as the number of objects in that category, divided by the total number of objects in all categories. If there are 10 pitchers, 7 of whom are right-handed and 3 left-handed, the proportion of players that are right-handed is $7/10 = .70$, and the proportion that are left-handed is $3/10 = .30$. The sum of the proportions in all mutually exclusive and exhaustive categories is always 1.00.

A proportion simply converts the frequency to a baseline of 1. In the above example, 3 out of 10 pitchers were left-handed; therefore, left-handedness occurs at a "rate" of .3 left-handers per pitcher. *Proportions are not percentages.* A percentage has a baseline of 100. Multiplying the proportion of left-handers by 100 would result in 30 percent, which is interpreted as 30 out of 100 being left-handed. We could multiply by an arbitrary value. For example, there would be $.3 \times 150 = 45$ left-handed pitchers per 150 pitchers.

Proportions are valuable for comparing frequencies in which the number of cases differs. For example, one team has a farm system of 138 pitchers, 41 of whom are left-handed, and the other a farm system of 149 pitchers, 44 left-handed. By dividing the number of left-handed pitchers in each case by the total number of pitchers, we find that the proportion of left-handers in the first farm system was $41/138 = .30$, or 30 percent, and the proportion in the other was $44/149$, which is also .30, or 30 percent. Even though the frequencies are different, the proportion of southpaws in the two groups is the same.

However, there is nothing inherent in a proportion that says that it is a "better" measure than frequency. They are simply different. Proportions measure the *rate* of occurrence of an event; frequencies measure the number of times the event occurred.

The Mean

A group of numbers is always located somewhere. Location does not mean their physical location, as in the press box or in the league president's office, but what the numbers are in relation to other numbers. A player's weight is usually located between 150 and 250 pounds. The location of a set of numbers is best indicated by their *central tendency,* or average—in a sense, the middle of the set. The word *average* has no technical meaning but is a general term referring to central tendency. The *mean,* the most useful of several measures of central tendency, is defined arithmetically as the sum of the values, divided by their number. If five players had 18, 23, 26, 37, and 42 home runs, respectively, the mean number of home runs would be obtained by summing the five values and dividing by 5:

$$Mean = (18 + 23 + 26 + 37 + 42) / 5 = 146 / 5 = 29.2$$

If the mean is subtracted from each individual score and the differences summed, the result will always be zero. The mean is therefore the balance point of a set of numbers. It is like a teeter-totter on which several objects are placed at different distances from the fulcrum. To remain balanced, the sum of the distances from the fulcrum in one direction must add up to the sum of the distances in the other:

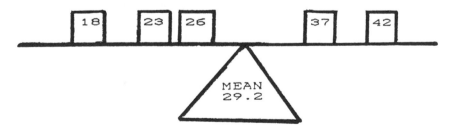

Because the mean is a balance point, it is sensitive to all of its values. If you change any one value (move one object on the teeter-totter), the mean will change. The location of a particular change does not matter. If any one of the objects is moved down the board by one foot, the mean will drop because the mean is based entirely on the sum, and no matter which value changes, the sum will change the same amount. On the other hand, the mean is greatly affected by the presence of an extreme score or two. If we had five players, four of whom hit 1, 2, 3, and 4 home runs and the fifth hit 50, the mean would be 60 / 5, or 12, despite the fact that none of the players was very close to this number. In this case, the mean is not a very realistic indication of where the numbers are located.

When there are one or two extreme values, the middle score, the *median,* may be more useful. Usually the median can be found by ranking the numbers and counting off half of them. The median number of home runs for the five players is the third highest (or lowest) value, 26. If there are an even number of values, the median may be taken to be halfway between the two middle ones.

The Standard Deviation

A second property of a set of numbers is that they differ from one another. They may differ by a large amount (i.e., they are scattered about), or they may cluster together. The degree of scattering is called *variability.* For example, if five players had home run totals of 10, 18, 26, 42, and 50, it is clear that they differ from one another more than those of five players who had 24, 26, 29, 31, and 35 home runs. The former group is therefore more variable.

The degree of variability in a set of values is measured by the *standard deviation.* Arithmetically, the standard deviation is defined as the square root of the sum of the squared deviations from the mean. That is a real mouthful, but it is not as imposing as it looks. The critical part of the standard deviation is the difference between each value in the set and the mean. The individual values will differ more from the mean when they are more variable; that is, when they differ more from one another. It is the size of these differences that determines the size of the standard deviation.

Computation of the standard deviation (SD):

1. Compute the mean by summing the values and dividing by their number.
2. For each value, subtract the mean from that value.
3. Square each of the differences.
4. Sum those values (the result is called the *sum of squares;* it is really the sum of squared differences).
5. Divide by the number of values (the result is called the *variance*).
6. Obtain the square root of the variance. This is the *standard deviation.*

Here are the calculations for the home runs hit by the two groups of players described above:

Group 1	Deviation	Square	Group 2	Deviation	Square
10	− 19.2	368.64	18	− 11.2	125.44
18	− 11.2	125.44	23	− 6.2	38.44
26	− 3.2	10.24	26	− 3.2	10.24
42	12.8	163.84	37	7.8	60.84
50	20.8	432.64	42	12.8	163.84
Sum 146	0	1100.80	146	0	398.80

Mean = 29.2 Variance = 220.16   Mean = 29.2 Variance = 79.76

SD = 14.84   SD = 8.93

The result confirms what was obvious from the values themselves. The standard deviation of the first group was higher (i.e., the players were more variable).

Actually, it is easier to compute the sum of squared deviations (sum of squares) directly from the original values rather than by subtracting the mean from each other. It also avoids compounding any rounding error. To obtain the sum of squares, simply square each value and add up those squares. Then square the sum of the values, divide by the number of values in the set, and subtract it from the first quantity. For Group 1, above:

$$SS = (10^2 + 18^2 \ldots + 50^2 = 100 + 324 \ldots + 2500 - (146^2 / 5)$$
$$= 5364 - 4263.20 = 1100.8$$

This is exactly the same value as was obtained by computing the sum of squares from each difference. This method will be used henceforth to compute sums of squares. This is an important computational formula, one you should become familiar with. The sum of squares (SS) is used frequently in statistical analysis. Remember too what SS represents: the sum of the squared deviations from the mean. The mean of the sum of squares is the variance (Var), and the square root of the variance is the standard deviation (SD). These three related measures are perhaps the most important measures in statistical analysis.

The larger the standard deviation, the more variable the values. But why do we go to all of the trouble of computing a standard deviation? Would it not be simpler just to average the deviations (taking absolute values, of course, because the algebraic sum will always be zero)? The true answer to this question is buried in the mathematics of statistics, but the practical advantage lies in the fact that the standard deviation possesses some very useful properties. For one thing, it is in the same units as the original values—in this case, the units of home runs. A standard deviation of 8.93 represents 8.93 home runs. This means that a player who hits 9 more or 9 fewer home runs than the mean of 29 deviates from the mean by about 1 standard deviation. This is important because *at least* 95 percent of the players will be within 2 standard deviations of the mean, that is, between $29 + 18 = 47$ and $29 - 18 = 11$ home runs. The mean and standard deviation indicate where the values lie (what their central point is) and provide an approximate idea of their range. Therefore, if you know the mean and standard deviation of a set of numbers, you know a lot about them.

It is possible to compute the mean of proportions as well. In fact, you can compute the mean of any set of numbers, no matter what they represent. In most cases the mean of a set of proportions will not equal the *overall* proportion if the denominators of the proportions are different. Suppose there are two groups of pitchers. One group consists of 2 pitchers, 1 of whom is left-handed. The other group consists of 8 pitchers, 2 left-handed. Combining the groups, there would be 10 pitchers, 3 left-handed, for an overall proportion of .30. The individual proportions, however, would be .50 in the first group and .25 in the second group. The mean of the two proportions is $.50 + .25 = .75 / 2 = .375$. In computing the mean, each group contributes equally. We simply add up the proportions irrespective of how many cases were involved in computing each one. In the overall proportion, a group contributes to the final result according to the number of cases.

Correlation Coefficients

In addition to measures of central tendency and variability, one other general statistic is important. It measures the degree of relationship between two sets of values. Suppose a set of five players is listed in order of the number of hits each player obtained in a seven-game World Series. Then the same five players are listed in order of the number of hits they obtained in the regular season. If the two lists look the same, that is, the order of the players is the same on both lists, the two sets of values (World Series hits and season hits) are said to be *positively correlated*. If one list is the reverse of the other (the players who had the most World Series hits had the fewest season hits), the two sets of values are said to be *negatively correlated*. If there is no consistency between one list and the other, the values are *uncorrelated*.

The statistic that measures the degree of correlation is called the *correlation coefficient*. There are several different kinds of correlation coefficients. Two of them will be illustrated.

Rank-Order Correlation

One easily computed measure of correlation is the rank-order correlation coefficient, or *rho*. The reason it is called the rank-order correlation is that it is concerned with the order of the values, not the actual values.

For example, consider the following five players from the Minnesota Twins, the number of hits they obtained in the 1987 World Series, and hits during the regular 1987 season:

Gaetti	7	150
Gagne	6	116
Gladden	9	109
Hrbek	5	136
Puckett	10	207

Begin by placing the World Series scores in order, from the highest to the lowest. Thus Puckett is number 1, Gladden is number 2, etc., until you get to Hrbek, number 5. If two players have the same value, each gets the same score, which is the sum of the two ranks, divided by 2. For example, if two players had the third highest score, they would be tied for ranks 3 and 4, and each would get a score of $(3+4)/2 = 7/2 = 3.5$. These ranks are to be correlated with the players' ranking on the number of hits obtained during the regular season. Therefore, the next step is to obtain the rank for each player for the regular season. Puckett is again 1, Gaetti, 2, etc.

The computation of *rho* then proceeds as follows:

1. List the rank on World Series hits for each player.
2. List the rank on season hits for each player.
3. Subtract the second rank from the first in each case.
4. Square the differences, and sum the squares.
5. Multiply the sum of the squares by 6.
6. Divide the above by the number of values, *cubed,* minus the number of values.
7. Subtract from 1.00.

	WS	Seas.	Diff.	Squares
Puckett	1	1	0	0
Gladden	2	5	+3	9
Gaettl	3	2	1	1
Gagne	4	4	0	0
Hrbek	5	3	2	4
Sum			0	14

$$\text{rho} = 1 - (6 \times 14) / (5^3 - 5) = 1 - (84 / 120) = 1 - .70 = .30$$

All correlation coefficients, including *rho*, vary from +1.00 to −1.00. The correlation will be +1.00 only if the ranks perfectly correspond, so that every difference is zero. The numerator is then zero, leaving *rho* as $1 + 0$. As the ranks become more and more discrepant, the numerator will increase, and the correlation coefficient will drop until it eventually becomes negative. It is not so obvious, but true, that the numerator will be largest when the ranks are perfectly inverted and will be twice the denominator. *Rho* will then equal $1 − 2$, or −1.00. A correlation of .30 is therefore positive, but nothing to write home about.

The Product-Moment Correlation Coefficient

This value, known as *r*, instead of using just the ranks, uses the values themselves. It is so commonly used that the term *correlation coefficient* means *r* unless it is otherwise specified. The computation of *r*, however, involves considerably more effort.

The measure *r* is a ratio. The numerator (the *sum of cross products*) is computed as follows:

1. Multiply each score by its counterpart. Sum those products.
2. Add up the World Series hits. Add up the season hits. Multiply the two sums and divide by the number of pairs or players.
3. Subtract the second value from the first.

$$SCP = (7 \times 150) + (6 \times 116) \ldots + (10 \times 207) - (37 \times 718) / 5 = 5477 - 5313.2 = 163.8$$

Remember, I said that the sum of squares was an important statistic. Here is another example. The denominator for *r* consists of the square root of the products of the sums of squares of the two measures. The sums of squares are computed just as they were in obtaining the standard deviation. For each set of five scores,

1. Square each value, and sum the squared values.
2. Square the sum, and divide it by the number of pairs.
3. Subtract each of these from the appropriate sum of squared scores.
4. Multiply those two values, and take the square root.

$$SS \ (\text{World Series}) = 10^2 + 9^2 + \ldots + 5^2 - 37^2 / 5 = 17.2$$

$$SS \ (\text{season}) = 207^2 + 109^2 + \ldots + 136^2 = 109{,}182 - 718^2 / 5 = 6077.2$$

Denom = SQRT (17.2 × 6077.2) = 323.3*

$r = 163.8 / 323.3 = .51$

The correlation is still positive but not overly large. *Rho* and *r* will usually not result in the same correlation since different information is being used in each case; *r* is a somewhat more precise measure since it uses more information than just the ranks.

The correlation coefficient is an extremely versatile tool. There are very few restrictions on when it may be applied. Any two things may be correlated, providing the two things may be appropriately paired. There is one important point, however. Correlation coefficients indicate the degree of *linear correlation*. Linearity measures the degree to which differences in one measure are proportional to differences in the other. If two measures are perfectly correlated, the difference between any two players in one measure will be a constant proportion of the difference in the other measure. If the relationship between the two measures is not at least approximately linear, *r* underestimates the true correlation.

The size of the correlation coefficient also depends on the range of values being correlated. If the range of values is small, the correlation is reduced. It is easy to see why this occurs. When the values within one set of numbers are very close together, even a small amount of irregularity in the second set will scramble the order badly. If the differences between the values are large, a great deal of irregularity can exist without changing the ranking.

---

*There are a number of equivalent computational procedures for obtaining r. One of the simplest is as follows:

1. *Compute the variance (standard deviation squared) for each of the two sets of numbers.*
2. *Add the two numbers making up each pair. Compute the variance of the sums.*
3. *Subtract both of the individual variances from the variance of the sums.*
4. *Divide by 2 times the product of the two standard deviations.*

$$r = (Var(x + y) - Var(x) - Var(y))/(2 \times SD(x) \times SD(y))$$

3

Single Categories

Statistical comparisons may be made between players on frequencies in single categories or frequencies in combinations of categories. This chapter begins by examining comparisons made on a single category such as singles or runs batted in. Batting, pitching, and fielding data are dealt with in somewhat different ways and will be considered separately.

The Batting Line

Here again is the modified batting line for Tony Gwynn in 1988:

											Total	Scoring			Steals		
PA	1B	2B	3B	HR	BB	HP	SH	SF	SO	DP	Out	Outs	R	NR	RBI	Att	SB	CS
578	129	22	5	7	51	0	4	2	40	11	307	358	64	514	70	37	26	11

It is difficult to interpret frequencies because a player does not have the same number of plate appearances as other batters and does not have the same number of plate appearances in different seasons. For example, in 1989 the year after he achieved the above record, Gwynn had 145 singles, but it took him 101 more plate appearances to obtain the additional 16 singles. The generally accepted argument is that he did not have as many opportunities to hit singles (or anything else) in 1988 as he had in 1989. The fewer number of singles could be a result of fewer chances rather than his batting prowess. It is especially unfair to compare the numbers because the batter has little control over the number of plate appearances. He may play less because of injuries or the manager's decision, or he may come to the plate less often because he is batting lower in the batting order or his team-mates do not get on base often enough to prolong the game.

Therefore, the values in the batting line could be more easily compared if they were expressed as a proportion of the total opportunities. The proportions are obtained by dividing the frequency in each of the exhaustive and mutually exclusive categories for plate appearances by the total.

The revised batting line would then look like this:

1B	2B	3B	HR	BB	HP	SH	SF	SO	DP	Out	Total
.223	.038	.009	.012	.088	.000	.007	.003	.069	.019	.531	1.000

Since the categories are exhaustive, the proportions are additive and sum to 1.000. These simple statistics do not depend on any assumption about baseball or the validity of any category. The proportions simply provide a measure of the rate at which the various events occur per plate appearance.

But that is not the whole story. Some of the times the batter faces the pitcher, he is deprived by circumstances of an opportunity to hit safely. Thus was born baseball's most primitive statistic: the official at-bat (AB). The rationale behind the official at-bat was briefly discussed in Chapter 1. Essentially, it means that part of the batting line is again rewritten to include only those plate appearances that are official (i.e., it excludes the plate appearances that resulted in bases on balls, hit by pitcher, sacrifice hits, and sacrifice flies under the assumption that those events are not under a batter's control). When talking about at-bats, it is as if the other events do not exist. What is left is a rather "deprived"-looking batting line that includes only singles, doubles, triples, home runs, and the three kinds of outs (i.e., the exhaustive and mutually exclusive categories of at-bats). It is no longer appropriate to include the other categories because some or all of those events occur on plate appearances that are not official at-bats.

The purpose of considering a particular portion of plate appearances, then, is to express various quantities in the batting line as a proportion of that subset. Dividing each frequency by the total at-bats results in the following for Gwynn's batting line:

AB	1B	2B	3B	HR	SO	DP	Out	Total
521	.248	.042	.010	.013	.077	.021	.589	1.000

Converting to proportions does not merely produce cosmetic changes but may make a considerable difference in how we evaluate a player's performance. Hank Aaron has hit more career home runs (755) than any other player in major league history, but proportionally he stands no better than thirteenth among players with over 4000 career at-bats with .061 home runs per at-bat. Proportions based on at-bats, however, are no longer theoretically neutral. Proportions of plate appearances simply serve a statistical function of "adjusting" frequencies to a common baseline, but proportions based on at-bats depend upon the assumptions that were responsible for defining that subset of plate appearances. Whether those assumptions create an interesting or useful subset is not a statistical matter. The statistic merely tells you about the numbers. What those numbers represent is debatable at another level.

Each of the above proportions may be expressed in other ways. For example, they may be expressed as percentages by multiplying each value by 100. Gwynn's percentage of home runs then becomes 1.3 percent, which means 1.3 home runs in 100 at-bats. A batter who plays a full season may expect about 600 at-bats. Therefore, the proportion may be expressed to a base of 600 by multiplying the proportion by 600. Thus Gwynn hit $.013 \times 600 = 7.8$ home runs per 600 at-bats. If Gwynn played the entire season, he should have hit about 8 home runs. Finally, the same frequencies may be reported as a reciprocal of the proportion by dividing at-bats by the frequency. The result is the number of at-bats per home run. Thus Gwynn required 521/7 or 74.4 at-bats for every home run. It is sometimes intuitively easier to grasp the meaning of a proportion's reciprocal than the proportion itself, and some frequencies are occasionally reported that way.

If sacrifice bunts are eliminated from plate appearances to form a subset called *official plate appearances,* they too are no longer theoretically neutral because we have assumed something about sacrifice bunts to define the official plate appearance. Bases on balls, hit by pitcher, and sacrifice flies may now be expressed as proportions of official plate appearances.

Dividing these quantities by at-bats does not produce proportions. Walks are not a subset of at-bats, and in fact no walk can occur on an at-bat. One can compute a ratio of any two quantities, but they are proportions only when they result from apportioning a set of events into mutually exclusive categories. If an entire batting line is expressed in appropriate proportions, with some quantities being proportions of at-bats and others as proportions of plate appearances, both sets are legitimate, but the total will not add up to 1.000. The proper way of expressing a mixed batting line would be

AB	1B	2B	3B	HR	SO	DP	Out	Total
521	.248	.042	.010	.013	.077	.021	.589	1.000

PA	BB	HP	SF	AB	Total
574	.089	.000	.003	.908	1.000

The total for each subset of total plate appearances is 1.000. Sacrifice bunts were not included in plate appearances in this case. This has little effect on the proportions since Gwynn had only 4 sacrifice bunts that season. Using the full complement of plate appearances has virtually no effect on the proportions.

So far, there has been no mention of the frequencies in the scoring categories. Runs may be expressed as a proportion of plate appearances and produces this line:

PA   R   NR
578 .111 .889

Scoring–not scoring represents an independent way of categorizing plate appearances. Therefore, this proportion is a separate accounting of those appearances. Furthermore, a player may drive in from 0 to 4 runs on each plate appearance. Therefore, the ratio of runs batted in to plate appearances is a mean of those values. In 1988, Gwynn batted in 70 / 578 = .121 runs per plate appearance. The denominator in this case should include sacrifice flies since runs batted in on those plate appearances resulting in sacrifice flies was included in the numerator. The necessary quantities for computing the mean are available from the official batting line: the sum of runs batted in on all plate appearances and the number of plate appearances. Do not confuse means with proportions just because the mean is less than 1.000. In theory, a batter could have 4.000 runs batted in per plate appearance if he hit a grand-slam home run every time he came to the plate.

Stolen bases are treated the same as runs batted in, as means, although it is possible to compute the proportion of attempted steals that are successful. For Gwynn, that proportion is 26 / 37 = .703. The *mean* number of stolen bases per plate appearance was 26 / 578 = .045.

Subsets of plate appearances other than at-bats may also be of interest. For example, consider the subset formed by adding strikeouts, double plays, and other outs. Each of the components is then a proportion of the total number of outs: strikeouts / outs = 40 / 358 = .112; double plays / outs = 11 / 358 = .031; other outs = .857, the remainder). A similarly interesting subset might be formed by combining the various hits and expressing singles, doubles, and triples as a proportion of hits (e.g., the proportion of hits that were home runs was 7 / 163 = .043). Statistically, any proportion is a legitimate expression, but whether it is interesting or valuable depends mostly on logical rather than statistical assumptions.

The Pitching Line

We have noted that the official pitching line consists of two very different components—that based on games and that based on batters faced. When a pitcher completes his part of the game, several entries are made. Therefore, that part of the pitching line may be divided into various parts, each of which represents a different subset of games. It is possible to express many of the quantities in this part of the pitching line as a proportion of either all or some subset of games to compensate for differences in mound appearances. Whether this is desirable depends upon whether one wishes to express the value as a "rate of occurrence" or simply make comparisons of the frequencies.

This part of Stieb's pitching line in frequencies looked like this:

	Games							Decisions				
Tot	GS	CG	IG	GR	GF	NF		Tot	W	L	S	ND	Sho
32	31	8	23	1	1	0		24	16	8	0	8	4

Various proportions that may be derived from this:

- Proportion of starts (31 / 32 = .969); proportion relieved (1 / 32 = .031).
- Proportion of starts completed (8 / 31 = .258); proportion not completed (23 / 31) = .742).
- Proportion of relief appearances finished (1 / 1 = 1.000).
- Proportion of games receiving decision (24 / 32 = .750); proportion of no decisions (8 / 32 = .250).
- Proportion of decisions won (16 / 24 = .667); proportion lost (8 / 24 = .333); proportion of saves (.000).

The more interesting part of the pitching line, however, is that based on individual batters faced. Batters faced is the exact counterpart of plate appearances for a batter.

			Plate Appearances								Scoring			
Player	BF	HR	OH	BB	HB	SH	SF	Outs	SO	Out		NR	R	ER	UR
Stieb	844	15	142	79	13	0	4	591	147	444		768	76	70	6

Misc.		
IP	WP	BK
207	4	5

Except that singles, doubles, and triples are included in the single category other hits (OH) and double plays are included in outs, this data line is identical to that for a batter and may be treated the same way. Some published data list the individual extra-base hits and results of attempted steals against some pitchers. When these data are available, the pitching line becomes an exact counterpart of the batting line.

Statistically, there is little that need be added. Quantities may be expressed as proportions of a pitcher's batters faced, just as for a batter's plate appearances. Some of the categories may also be expressed as a proportion of at-bats and commonly are, but the practice seems based on a desire to provide equivalent statistics for batters and pitchers rather than a sound rationale. Bases on balls and so on may be interpreted as neutral to a batter but are self-inflicted by a pitcher, and the subset of at-bats is therefore inherently less interesting.

The question of what to do with sacrifices also opens a whole new set of considerations. Actually, there is a good theoretical reason to omit intentional bases on balls from plate appearances than other quantities (when those numbers are available). Sacrifices, sacrifice flies, and intentional walks are about 25 percent more common in the National League but occur on less than 3 percent of the total batters faced and may have little effect on the totals.

Here is Stieb's pitching line in proportional form:

PA	OH	HR	SH	SF	HB	BB	SO	Out	Total	Runs	ER	ER/R
844	.168	.018	.000	.005	.015	.094	.174	.526	1.000	.090	.083	.922

Runs is proportionalized on batters faced as well, since each batter faced scores or does not. Earned runs may also be expressed as a proportion of batters faced or total runs. Runs divided by the number of batters reaching base (H + HR + BB + HB) appears to be a proportion but is not because some runners that reach base (e.g., on errors) are categorized as out. This ratio may be interesting but should not be treated as if it were a proportion.

Very little may be done with wild pitches and balks. They are not a subset of anything readily identifiable, except perhaps runners reaching base, and are relatively infrequent.

The Fielding Line

With the exception of double plays, the sum of putouts, assists, and errors provides a basis for expressing any of the three as a proportion of the total. The only one of interest, however, is the proportion of errors, which is usually reported as its inverse, the proportion of nonerrors (successfully fielded chances), and is known as the *fielding average*. Statistically, this has the effect of permitting comparisons of error rates when total chances differ widely.

Another widely used procedure is to divide the entries in the fielding line by games played. While this creates a legitimate set of means, the interpretation is somewhat ambiguous. A game played is the same for a regular player who takes his position for nine full innings and a defensive replacement who may play only an inning or two. This problem could be easily corrected by using innings played as a denominator, but these data are not available in official summaries.

Summary

While the proportion and mean are both computed by dividing frequencies by at-bats or plate appearances, the distinction between the two measures is not trivial. As we shall see, the kind of statistical analysis and its interpretation often depends upon the form of a particular ratio.

4

Derived Statistics

One of the functions of statistics is to summarize data, to reduce a lot of numbers to a few numbers that describe the important properties of the larger set. Statistics designed to describe the performance of a particular player are therefore usually formed by combining frequencies in various categories. These statistics will be called *derived statistics*. Any derived statistic has two elements: the categories that are used in its construction and the rule by which those categories are combined (i.e., addition, subtraction, multiplication, division, etc.). The number of possible combinations of categories and the ways they may be combined, while not infinite, is very large. There is usually some reason for selecting the components and the combination rule. It makes very little sense to add the number of times a batter is hit by a pitch to the number of times he hits into double plays and divide by his number of triples.

In this chapter, several compound measures will be considered. The survey is not intended to be exhaustive in either a historical or a contemporary sense but illustrative of the statistical properties of particular kinds of combinations. The discussion will focus on statistics derived from the batting line. In most cases, the same statistic is computable from the pitching line. Exceptions will be noted. Fielding will be considered separately.

Derived statistics fall into a few broad categories: unweighted or weighted sums of proportions, unweighted or weighted sums of frequencies, simple ratios or sums of ratios, multiplicative combinations, and undifferentiated ratios. Each of these has unique statistical properties.

Summed Proportions

Some of the most useful statistics are formed by simply summing the proportions in various categories. These may be *unweighted* (each category contributes equally) or *weighted* (some categories are weighted to give them more importance). Sometimes plate appearances is used as a baseline for these proportions, and sometimes at-bats is used. The proportions computed for Gwynn's 1988 season will again be used as an example. The necessary proportions for both plate appearances and at-bats are as follows:

PA	1B	2B	3B	HR	BB	HP	SH	SF	SO	DP	Out*	Total
578	.223	.038	.009	.012	.088	.000	.007	.003	.069	.019	.531	1.000

AB	1B	2B	3B	HR	SO	DP	Out*	Total
521	.248	.042	.010	.013	.077	.021	.589	1.000

Unweighted Sums

The Batting Average. The *batting average* is the sum of the unweighted proportions of singles, doubles, triples, and home runs per at-bat. Gwynn's batting average is

$$BA = .248 + .042 + .010 + .013 = .313$$

Because the denominator is the same for each proportion, the batting average is more conveniently computed by summing the frequencies and dividing by the common denominator, at-bats. This also avoids cumulating the rounding errors in the component proportions.

$$BA = (129 + 22 + 5 + 7) = 163 / 521 = .313$$

Descriptively, the batting average is nothing more than the proportion of hits. Since bases on balls, hit by pitcher, sacrifices, and sacrifice flies are excluded from both the numerator and denominator, the "other part" of the proportion reduces to (AB – H) = outs. Subtracting the batting average from 1.000 yields the proportion of at-bats resulting in outs. The batting average is occasionally maligned as a measure of batting success because it values every hit the same (i.e., a single counts as much as a home run). To some extent, this is a bad rap. The flip side of the batting average is the *outs average*. It is important for a batter to avoid making outs, whatever else he may do, since a team is allowed only 27 outs in a game. In this sense, the batting average is a measure of the tendency to avoid making outs. It is trivial but true that the batting average is not a percentage despite being abbreviated Pct. in many summaries.

On-Base Average. A second common statistic that is the sum of

---

Outs excluding strikeouts and double plays but including fielder's choice and safe on errors. Plate appearances include sacrifice bunts.

unweighted proportions is the *on-base average,* sometimes mistakenly called the *on-base percentage.* The on-base average is the sum of the unweighted proportions of each of the events that allow a batter to reach base (singles, doubles, triples, home runs, bases on balls, and hit by pitcher). The baseline for on-base average is plate appearances (less sacrifice bunts). For Gwynn, the on-base average is

$$OB = .225 + .038 + .009 + .012 + .089 = .373$$

Like the batting average, it may also be more conveniently computed by summing the frequencies of on-base events and dividing by plate appearances (less sacrifice bunts).

$$OB = (163 + 51) = 214 / 574 = .373$$

A player's on-base average will be higher than his batting average. This is an arithmetic consequence of adding the same sum (bases on balls and hit by pitcher) to the numerator and denominator of a ratio. Adding the proportion of bases on balls and hit by pitcher to the batting average will not yield the on-base average. The denominator for the components of on-base average is plate appearances; the denominator for the individual quantities in the batting average is at-bats.

The on-base average does not tell you how often the player was really on base because it does not include the number of times he reached base on an error or fielder's choice. Therefore, the ratio of runs scored to the numerator of the on-base average is not a proportion. Some runs are scored when the batter does not "officially" reach base.

Weighted Sums

Two counterparts to the batting average and on-base average also consist of the sum of proportions, but in this case each proportion is weighted by the number of bases attained.

Slugging Average. This statistic, like the batting average, is the sum of the proportions of singles, doubles, triples, and home runs per at-bat, but each proportion is weighted by the number of bases attained on that hit. For Gwynn, this would be

$$SA = (1 \times .248) + (2 \times .042) + (3 \times .010) + (4 \times .013) = .248 + .084 + .030 + .052 = .414$$

The slugging average may also be computed by appropriately weighing the frequencies in each category, summing the weighted frequencies to get *total bases,* and dividing by at-bats:

$$SA = (1 \times 129) + (2 \times 22) + (3 \times 5) + (4 \times 7) = 216 / 521 = .415$$

Slugging average is not in itself a proportion. One does not get credit for a total base or no total base on each at-bat. Despite the fact that the slugging average is seldom greater than 1.000, it could have a maximum of 4.000 (a home run on every at-bat). Slugging average may also be thought of as a mean. The mean is computed by summing the total bases obtained on each at-bat (0, 1, 2, 3, or 4) and dividing by the number of at-bats. In essence, it is the mean number of bases gained by batting per at-bat.

Total Offense. The weighted counterpart of on-base average may be called *total offense*. This statistic is the summed proportions of bases on balls, hit by pitcher, each weighted as +1 and added to the weighted proportions of singles, doubles, triples, and home runs—all based on plate appearances (not at-bats). For the example case, this would be

$$TOFF = (1 \times .225) + (2 \times .038) + (3 \times .009) + (4 \times .012) + (1 \times .089) = .465$$

Likewise, the measure may be computed by adding the frequencies of bases on balls and hit by pitcher to total bases to form a quantity called *bases gained*, which is then divided by plate appearances:

$$TOFF = 216 + 51 = 267 / 574 = .465$$

Bases gained may include stolen bases (weighted +1) and caught stealing (weighted −1). Strictly speaking, neither is part of the proportional components of plate appearances, but computationally this is of no consequence. Total offense, like slugging average, is not in itself a proportion because of the weighting of components. The addition of the consequences of attempted stolen bases does not change the metric properties of the statistic. It is essentially mean bases gained per plate appearance.

Isolated Power. The basic structure of a statistic may often be hidden by a shortcut computational procedure. One such statistic is *isolated power*. Some sources state that isolated power is the slugging average minus the batting average. That is true, but that description hides the true relationship between slugging average and isolated power. More properly, isolated power is the sum of the same four proportions used in computing the slugging average, except that each proportion is weighted by the number of *extra bases* attained by that event rather than total bases. Therefore, singles are weighted by 0, doubles by 1, triples by 2, and home runs by 3. Isolated power may be thought of as the weighted proportion of these three events or as the mean number of extra bases per at-bat. Gwynn's isolated power is

$$IP = (1 \times .042) + (2 \times .010) + (3 \times .013) = .101$$

Like the slugging average, it may be computed by weighting each of the individual frequencies by the number of extra bases, summing the weighted totals to get total extra bases, and dividing by at-bats.

Summed Frequencies

A valid argument may be made that a player's contribution to offense is determined by not just what he does but how often he does it. Therefore, it is not mandatory to divide by plate appearances. A player who hits 24 home runs contributes more than a player who hits 12 home runs, even if it takes him twice as many plate appearances to do so. Following this reasoning, total hits, total times reaching base safely, total bases, or bases gained are valid measures of offensive production without casting them into ratio form.

Batting Runs. Bases gained (the expanded version of total bases), like total bases, is simply a weighting of the outcomes of each plate appearance by the number of bases attained by that outcome. The most sophisticated measures of total offense are those that weight each event not by the actual bases gained but by a weighting factor that reflects the run-scoring potential of that event.

Run-scoring potential is a complicated concept, but basically it works like this. Every time a particular combination of runners on base and outs occurs (e.g., runner on first, no outs; or runners on first and third, two outs), a certain number of runs will score. Exactly how many may be determined by examining the situations in thousands of games and averaging the total runs resulting from each situation. Also, each event (single, home run, walk, etc.) contributes to the occurrence of each runners-outs situation. In other words, *x* percent of the singles result in a runner on first and two out; another *y* percent result in a runner on first and third and no outs, and so on. By considering how and how often each event changes the runners-outs situation from one value to another, we can arrive at a number that reflects the average number of runs produced by a single, double, triple, and so on.

The metric advantage of this measure is obvious. The object of the offense is to score runs, and a measure of a batter's performance in those units rather some abstract unit like total bases would be directly interpretable.

Several procedures have been devised for obtaining the weights, most of which are tedious and complicated. They also require computer techniques and a data base that is considerably beyond that available to the average fan. The important thing is that weights are not just guesses. They are based on the actual results of thousands of games.

The most generally known system is the Linear Weights System (LWTS) published by Thorn and Palmer in *The Hidden Game of Baseball*. The authors give a detailed account and prescription for the use of their equation, but only the bare essentials will be presented here. Their equation is as follows:

Batting Runs = $(.46 \times 1B) + (.80 \times 2B) + (1.02 \times 3B) + (1.4 \times HR) + .33(BB + HP) + (.3 \times SB) - (.6 \times CS) - (a \times Outs)$

The equation means that a single is worth .46 runs; a double, .80 runs; a triple, 1.02 runs; and so on. There is one new quantity in the equation—*outs*. An out is considered to have a negative impact on potential runs scored; hence the weighted value of outs along with the weighted value for caught stealing is subtracted from the total created by the other events. In structure, *batting runs* is exactly equivalent to bases gained. The only difference is the weights.

There is one bit of added complexity in the LWTS system. The weighting for outs, appearing as *a* in the equation, is determined by how much offense exists in the group of players to which the batter belongs (usually all league batters in a given season). Their reasoning is that in a "batter's year," an out is more of a negative event than it is in a "pitcher's year"; therefore, *a* is an inverse function of league batting average.

Moreover, one can adjust the value of *a* so that the weighted value for outs is equal to the average value of the sum of all other components being considered. This means that a player who performs exactly at the group average in terms of the sum of individual events excluding outs, will have a value of zero batting runs when the weighted outs are subtracted.*

While adjusting the value of *a* does complicate the computational

---

The procedure for computing a *is actually quite simple. You need to find that value of* a *that will produce a league total of 0 batting runs. First, take the league totals except for outs and compute league batting runs by multiplying the number of events in each category by the appropriate weight and summing them exactly as you would for an individual player. Divide this total by the total number of outs for the league. The result is* a.

Example: The batting line for the American League in 1941 was as follows:

AB	1B	2B	3B	HR	BB	SB	CS
43125	8184	2066	508	734	4742	471	323

The Thorne-Palmer equation then gives

Batting Runs = $(.46 \times 8184) + (.8 \times 2066) + (1.02 \times 508) + (1.4 \times 734) + (.33 \times 4742) + (.3 \times 471) - (.6 \times 323) = 8475.56$

Outs = $43125 - 8184 - 2066 - 508 - 734 = 31633$

Therefore, a = *$8475.56 / 31633 = .268$*

procedure, it allows batting runs to be expressed as the number of potential runs produced by that batter above the number that would be produced by an average batter (i.e., runs above average). Negative runs (the weighted outs exceeds the positive contribution of total bases gained) means that the player is below the group average (i.e., he is performing worse than the average batter). It does not mean that he has a negative impact on the offense. The computation of batting runs is straightforward and as simple as computing total offense.

Here are the computations for Gwynn, using .25 as the value of *a:*

$$\text{Batting Runs} = (.46 \times 129) + (.8 \times 22) + (1.02 \times 5) + (1.4 \times 7) +$$
$$(.33 \times 51) + (.3 \times 26) - (.6 \times 11) - (.25 \times 358) =$$
$$59.3 + 17.6 + 5.1 + 9.8 + 16.8 + 7.8 - 6.6 - 89.5 = 20.3$$

Over the season, Gwynn's performance was worth 20.3 runs above the league average. This value reflects the *number* of runs, or the total offense contributed by a player, and is therefore influenced by the number of plate appearances. If each of the proportions was identical for two players, the final batting runs would be proportional to the difference in at-bats. Batting runs is usually not averaged but used as a measure of *amount* of offense.

The statistics in all three categories discussed so far share a very important property: The numerator may be obtained by assigning every plate appearance or at-bat a value and summing those values. In essence, they are additive statistics.

Simple and Summed Ratios

Some statistics are constructed by dividing a frequency by the frequency in some other category. Often both the numerator and denominator are mutually exclusive classes of the same larger set. Usually these ratios are ratios of good things to bad things or vice versa.

Strikeouts-Walks Ratio

The simple ratio of a pitcher's strikeouts to bases on balls is occasionally referred to in scouting reports. Walks and strikeouts are mutually exclusive results of batters faced. Together with hit batters, they make up an exhaustive categorization of those batters faced who do not put the ball in play. Their ratio is simply an index value. It is not a proportion because one of two mutually exclusive outcomes cannot be a proportion of another.

The Earned Run Average

Since the early part of the century, the *earned run average* has been used
as the primary statistic for evaluating pitcher effectiveness. We have already
discussed problems in the definition of an earned run and various inequities
in assigning to pitchers the responsibility for runs earned. But there is more
to come with respect to this venerable statistic.

The earned run average is essentially the ratio of earned runs allowed
to innings pitched. The ratio is multiplied by 9 to scale it to the level of a
game and make it more comprehensible, but that operation has nothing to
do with its statistical properties. Unlike the batting average, the on-base
average, and the slugging average, the earned run average is neither a proportion nor an average. It is simply another ratio of bad things to good things.

The problem with the earned run average lies in the definition of *inning
pitched.* Unlike the inning of a game, an inning pitched has no reality. A
pitcher receives credit for one-third of an inning pitched every time an out
is made while he is pitching (whether he has anything to do with it or not).
If he gets all three outs in one real inning or one out in each of three separate
games is of no consequence. In a very real sense, an inning pitched is defined by outs, not by innings, and the earned run average is a ratio of earned
runs to outs, multiplied by 27, not an *average* of earned runs allowed per
inning pitched.

In pitching as in batting, the result of each batter who comes to the plate
is recorded. From the pitcher's point of view, only a limited number of things
may happen. The batter may be put out (before or after reaching base), he
may score a run, or he may be left on base. Runs (hence earned runs) are
not included in outs any more than strikeouts are included in bases on balls.
They are both the outcome of a batter faced. Therefore, the ratio of runs to
outs is no more a proportion or average than the ratio of strikeouts to bases
on balls.

This does not mean that the earned run average is not a useful statistic.
It has proven its viability over the years. It is simply an index that expresses
a relationship between the number of outs (innings) and earned runs
allowed.

Total Average

The earned run average is essentially the ratio of bad things (runs) to
good things (outs). Occasionally, similar measures have been proposed for
batting. *Total average,* originated by Tom Boswell, is one of these. Total
average, at least in some forms, has bases gained as the numerator (the same
as total offense) but uses outs as the denominator rather than plate appear-

ances. Thus, for a batter, it is the ratio of good things to bad things. This has the effect of changing its metric properties, for like the earned run average, total average is neither a proportion nor a mean.

One variation on this theme for some indexes is to include sacrifices in the numerator and the denominator under the assumption that they are both good (advance a runner) and bad (make an out). The net result, however, is rather inconsistent.

If the ratio without sacrifices is less than 1.000, the value of the statistic increases as the proportion of sacrifices gets greater—a simple arithmetic consequence of adding the same amount to the numerator and denominator. When the denominator is 1.000, sacrifices will have no effect on total average, but they will reduce the total average when the ratio without them is more than 1.000.

A given number of sacrifices will also have a greater effect for smaller numbers of bases gained. Including sacrifices for a player with a low initial total average would help him more than a player who has a high total average. Whether this is desirable depends upon one's philosophy concerning sacrifices. Since the number of sacrifices is not completely dependent on the batter, a good argument could be made for eliminating them entirely. For most modern players, however, sacrifices provide such a low proportion of the total plate appearances that whatever is done with them is of little consequence.

5

Properties of
Derived Statistics

Additivity

Statistics composed of either unweighted or weighted sums of proportions (batting average, on-base average, slugging average, isolated power, total offense) are *additive*. Each is based on the sum of the outcomes of each plate appearance or at-bat. In other words, in computing batting average, the result of an at-bat is a hit (1) or not (0). Dividing the sum by the number of at-bats provides the batting average. This means that sets or subsets of at-bats are also additive.

The value of the statistic for a team is equal to the sum of the numerators for individual players, divided by the total plate appearances or at-bats for those players. Batting runs is also additive in this sense; the total number of batting runs is equal to the sum of the batting runs computed for each plate appearance. Not all statistics have this convenient property.

Ratios to Outs

When the denominator of a ratio is outs, the statistic is not based on the sum of the outcome for each out; that is, one cannot specify the value to be assigned to each out. Ratios such as the earned run average and total average are therefore not true averages. They are computationally additive—the numerator consists of the sum of positive events and the denominator consists of the sum of negative events for those plate appearances—but they are not additive with respect to the individual events in the denominator, as are statistics based on the sum of the outcomes of each plate appearance.

Production Index

This statistic is simply the sum of the slugging and on-base averages. Therefore, given the two components, the production index is exceptionally easy to compute, but because the two components have different denominators, adding the two ratios is somewhat like adding apples and monkey wrenches. It is not clear just what the final value represents. The situation is clarified somewhat by looking at the components. Each part consists of total hits plus another component. In one case, the "other" component is the number of total extra bases, and in the other it is the number of bases on balls plus the number of times hit by the pitcher.

The relationship of the overall production index to its individual plate appearances is complicated somewhat by the fact that the two components have different denominators. Each measure consists of an additive combination of components, but a combined production index based on combined players (e.g., a team) or combining various situations for a single player (e.g., home games vs. road games) must be computed by separately obtaining the slugging average and on-base average for the combined set and summing them. Summing the production indexes for the separate players does not make sense.

Example: In 1988, Wade Boggs had 164 total bases in 300 at-bats at home and 115 total bases in 321 at-bats on the road. He reached base safely 174 times in 366 plate appearances at home and 145 times in 376 plate appearances on the road. His overall production index is obtained by first computing the total slugging average $-(164+115)/(300+321)=279/621=$ .449$-$and the total on-base average$-(174+145)/(366+376)=319/742=$ .430. The production index is $.449+.430=.879$.

Multiplicative Ratios

When the numerator of a ratio statistic consists either in whole or in part of a multiplicative combination of components, additivity in any meaningful sense is destroyed. In addition, there are other special properties of such statistics that must be considered.

Speed-Power Ratio

The product of home runs and stolen bases divided by the sum of those quantities defines this statistic and provides a simple example of some properties of statistics with multiplicative numerators. Like any statistic in which the numerator is the product of two values, a player can achieve a high value on this statistic only by scoring well in both categories. A zero value in either reduces the ratio to zero, and a zero in both categories renders it noncomputable (division by zero). Bill James, who created this statistic, suggests that the numerator be doubled, but this has no effect on its metric properties. It simply increases the difference between players and reduces the likelihood of values less than 1.000.

More important, however, one cannot obtain team values by summing the numerator and denominator for the various players and computing the ratio. To obtain a team value for speed-power ratio, you have to obtain the sum of home runs and the sum of stolen bases separately before carrying out any of the other arithmetic operations, or the measure will not make sense.

Runs Created

This statistic, another creation of Bill James's, is a more complicated multiplicative ratio related to total offense. Runs created has been revised several times, and one must be careful to determine which version is referred to. In its ultimate form, it is similar to production index because it is a ratio determined primarily by two main components: times reaching base safely and total bases. It differs from production ratio in that the two values are multiplied to form the numerator. There is also a third component, which is additive. The denominator is plate appearances. The computation includes every component in the batting line except runs, runs batted in, and strikeouts. Despite its name, it is not like batting runs; it is not really in units of runs. Nor do the constants appear to have any theoretical basis.

The statistic is obtained by computing three quantities. The first quantity (A) is the number of times the player reaches base minus the times he is caught stealing and the times he hits into a double play. The second factor (B) is equal to total bases, plus .26 times the total of bases on balls, minus intentional bases on balls, plus hit by pitcher. The third factor (C) is equal to .52 times the sum of sacrifices, sacrifice flies, and stolen bases. The final value of runs created is simply $A \times B + C$, divided by plate appearances (including both sacrifices and sacrifice flies).

Since the final combination is divided by plate appearances, runs created resembles an additive statistic. Each of the three components is a weighted sum of the frequencies in various categories, and the total is divided by plate appearances. However, the total includes the multiplicative combination of A and B, so that the numerator is not simply the additive results of the runs created on each plate appearance.

As with the speed-power ratio, total runs created obtained by summing the numerators for subsets of plate appearances to get a value for the combined set is not appropriate. The overall value for the numerator must be obtained by first combining the frequencies in the individual categories, then computing the overall values for A, B, and C for those sums. The denominator is equal to the sum of the plate appearances for all subsets being combined. The reason for this procedure is strictly arithmetic. The sum of products is not equal to the product of the sums. Nonadditive statistics like runs created often produce bizarre results when numerators are computed for different sets, then summed. For example, the sum of the numerators for home and road games will be quite different from the numerator computed from the sums of the frequencies in each category.

Nonadditivity is not a critical problem with a statistic, and in fact the unique aspect of multiplicative components may be desirable in some cases. As we will see, however, additivity does have some statistical advantages.

Runs created has been a very useful measure of total offense. The several incarnations are specific to different years when the available data differ. The fact that the numerator is in part a product, however, requires a player to get on base a lot and hit for extra bases to obtain a high score. For Gwynn, runs created (the most complete version) is computed as follows:

$$A = 129 + 51 + 0 - 11 - 11 = 158$$
$$B = 216 + (.26 \times (51 - 13 + 0)) = 225.9$$
$$C = .52 \times (4 + 2 + 26) = 16.6$$
$$\text{Denominator} = \text{Plate Appearances} = 578$$
$$\text{Runs Created} = (158 \times 225.9 + 16.6) / 578 = 35,708.8 / 578 = 61.8$$

Special Problems

Pitching Measures

The apparent direct relevance of the earned run average to pitching effectiveness and the fact that many important categories are not reported in the official pitching line have probably made derived statistics for pitchers of less interest than those for batters. Nevertheless, if statistics based on the individual outcomes of plate appearances are useful indicators of the offensive contribution of batters, the same measures should indicate the effectiveness of pitching.

The computation of *opponents batting average* and *opponents on-base average* are easily carried out from the pitching line. However, problems arise with respect to the total offense measures because the pitching line lacks the breakdown of extra-base hits. This impoverishment may not prove as serious as it appears. Gill and Reeve, in their *Mathematics of Baseball,* suggest that total bases may be estimated from hits and home runs by the following procedure:

$$\text{Total Bases} = AB \times (.333 \times H + .693 \times HR) / IP$$

Although the authors state that the estimates are "fairly accurate," their actual accuracy is not known. Whether this proves the best possible estimate or not, the point is that in the absence of data one often can make do, and even an estimated figure may be satisfactory.

Example: In 1988, Jimmy Key of Toronto allowed 222 hits in 866 at-bats, of which 24 were home runs. According to the Gill-Reeve equation, the total bases should be:

$$TB = 866 \times [(.333 \times 222) + (.693 \times 24) / 232] = 866 \times .390 = 337.8$$

The slugging average (TB / AB) against Key is represented by the part in brackets (.390), and other measures that require total bases may be computed using the estimated value of 338.

Pitching Runs

Pitching runs, * the pitching counterpart of batting runs, may be computed, even though the individual extra base hits are not available. Thorn and Palmer suggest that multiplying total extra bases by .31 per extra base will be satisfactory. We have also omitted stolen-base data for this example. Key allowed 353 estimated total bases on 222 hits, for a total of $338 - 222 = 116$ extra bases. Key also walked 77 batters. Estimating the batting runs allowed by Key (pitching runs), we have

$$\text{Runs} = (.46 \times 222) + (.31 \times 116) + (.33 \times 77) - (.25 \times 644) = 2.5$$

How does this fare against Key's actual pitching runs? Key gave up 147 singles, 47 doubles, and 4 triples in addition to the 24 home runs in 1988. His actual pitching runs:

$$\text{Runs} = (.46 \times 147) + (.8 \times 47) + (1.02 \times 4) + (1.4 \times 24) + (.33 \times 77) - (.25 \times 644) = 7.3$$

*Do not confuse this measure with another statistic also known as *Pitching Runs.* That measure is essentially the difference between a pitcher's earned run average and that of the league for that season.*

In this case, the estimation was within five runs of the actual pitching runs allowed.

All of this may be too much approximation and not enough measurement for some tastes, but in the absence of the actual data, estimates are often the best that can be done. This is merely a computational example. Predictions for other players may not fare this well, and the validity of any particular estimation procedure must be ensured in a large number of cases before it can be put to general use.*

Fielding Measures

The fielding average is the ratio of errors to total chances. Although it is a legitimate proportion, it has been widely criticized. The late Branch Rickey, who pioneered the use of statistics in baseball management, once commented that nothing (statistical) could be done with fielding, and that is true. The problem does not lie in the lack of statistics but in the lack of meaningful data. Metrically, the fielding average is an unweighted proportion—the proportion of successfully fielded chances (1.000 minus the proportion of errors). The problems lie in the definition of a fielding chance and the relationship between measures and actual fielding performance. Those issues are matters of validity rather than statistical legitimacy and will be considered in a later chapter.

Range Factor

One of the simplest derived measures of fielding is obtained by summing the putouts, assists (and sometimes errors) to get total chances, then dividing this value by games played. The theory behind this measure is that a "good" fielder will accept more chances because he is able to reach more batted balls. The problem with games as a common denominator has been mentioned, but this is easily resolvable by computing chances as a ratio to team outs (innings). This creates a measure that appears to be like earned run average and total average, which are also ratios to outs, but the superficial similarity is misleading. In earned run average and total average, outs are defined by the player's actions. In this case, outs are defined independently of what the player does. The ratio of fielding chances (minus

---

*Gill and Reeve arrived at their estimation equation by a procedure called multiple regression, that guarantees that the two constants will give the best possible estimate. This procedure will be discussed in Chapter 11.

errors) to outs is the sum of two unweighted proportions (putouts and assists) because any fielder receives credit for a putout, an assist, or neither on every team out.* Thus, each out represents a possible fielding chance, and the three categories (putout, assist, and neither) represent mutually exclusive and exhaustive categories.

The basic ratio is essentially a proportion. In practice, however, *range factor* usually weights the two components differently for various positions, under the assumption that putouts or assists are more, or less, "difficult." For example, assists may be weighted more heavily and differently for the various infield positions. The weights appear to be arbitrary, however. This puts the range factor in the same category as slugging average, and so on. It is a weighted sum of proportions.

It is not clear, however, how range factor should be computed at the team level because the number of outs for a team is more or less constant for a season. Statistically, range factors may be added across players to get a team value, but there is not much sense in doing so.

General Properties of Compound Measures

The major purpose of computing a derived measure is to describe the differences among players. Once a statistic is computed, the players may be listed in order according to the values of that statistic. A derived statistic is interesting to the extent that it creates a different list; that is, it is uncorrelated with other statistics. Since there are only about a dozen or so categories that are used in most derived statistics, most statistics share categories with other statistics. No matter how they are weighted, statistics composed of the same categories will always be correlated to some extent.

The results of adding frequencies in various categories are fairly predictable. Even though merely adding them appears to weight each category equally, this is not so. There are two factors that will determine the differences between players: the standard deviation of the categories and the degree to which the categories are correlated with one another.

Standard Deviation

The category with the largest standard deviation will contribute more to differences between players. In the simplest case, the list of players based

---

*If errors are included, the measure simply becomes an undifferentiated ratio, because there is a quantity in the numerator that is not part of the denominator. There is also a minor inaccuracy introduced by run-down plays in which a player may receive both a putout and an assist on the same out.

on the sum of two measures will more closely resemble the list on the measure with the larger standard deviation—the one in which the players differ more from one another—than the list with the smaller standard deviation. This has nothing to do with the importance of that category. It is simply a consequence of the arithmetic. Moreover, if the measures are weighted in some way, the standard deviation of each measure is increased by a factor equivalent to multiplying it by the weight. It is these weighted standard deviations that will determine the final result.

Slugging average and on-base average have many categories in common. Because those categories are weighted in the case of slugging average, the standard deviation in slugging average is larger than that for on-base average. The production index, which is a simple sum of the two measures, will correlate more highly with slugging average than on-base average. If we listed players according to production index, we would get almost the same list that we get when we list them according to slugging average. The listing would differ quite a bit from that in which players are listed according to on-base average, however.

Slugging average is determined by total bases. The difference in total bases in turn is almost entirely determined by the difference in home runs. If we start by listing players according to slugging average and compare that list with one obtained with home runs removed from slugging average, the two lists would be completely different. On the other hand, removing singles, doubles, or triples from the slugging average should leave us with almost the same list. The standard deviation for home runs is not only larger than that for the other factors to begin with, but when each value is multiplied by 4 in obtaining total bases, it is increased by a factor of 4. Because of the large variability in total bases, most derived statistics that include total bases as an additive component are highly correlated, and the effect is largely a result of differences in home runs.

Despite its attractive theoretical derivation, the batting runs (LWTS) weighting system may not produce a list much different from one based on any of the other total-offense measures. Batting runs, when divided by plate appearances, will correlate very highly with total average and production index. Like its less sophisticated brethren, batting runs is largely determined by total bases and walks, and high correlations would be expected because the same categories are included in all measures. In addition, the different weights assigned to most categories in computing batting runs are almost proportional to the actual bases gained.*

Some publications seem to show that ranking players on Slugging Average or Total Average will not yield the same ranking as that obtained with Batting Runs. This may be misleading because such lists only consider a small range of batters, usually the top ten or twenty. By restricting the range, and only looking at a few cases it makes the measures appear to be more different than they really are. See Chapter 2.

Correlation

The other factor that determines the effect of adding one quantity to another is the correlation between the quantities. Adding two quantities that are positively correlated will not change the listing produced by either one separately. The lower the correlation between the two quantities, the greater the difference between the ranking of players according to the sum and the rankings on each of the two components separately. It makes little sense to rank players on the sum of home runs and runs batted in since the two lists are almost identical to begin with. Adding two quantities that are negatively correlated will tend to reduce any differences between players.

Correlations Between Derived Measures

The interpretation of high correlations between measures is not always straightforward, however. Correlations are seldom perfect, even when the number of shared categories is large, and often the few players that do not conform to the general pattern provide insight into those players' performances. For most players, stolen bases does not contribute much to total bases gained. For 90 percent of the players, it is less than 10 percent of the total. But a few players (Vince Coleman, Rickey Henderson) have an exceptionally large number of stolen bases.

Thus, whether stolen bases is included in bases gained will make little difference in the bases gained of most players but will have a substantial effect for those few players who run a lot. Overall, the correlation will be high between a measure of total offense that includes stolen bases and one that does not. The list of players, however, shows Henderson, Tim Raines, Kirk Gibson, and Gwynn to be in the top 10 when steals are included (Raines and Henderson are 1, 2), but they barely make the top 20 without thefts. The rest of the players do not change their position in the list by very much, hence the high correlation. The point is that there are other things to consider when making lists of players other than the correlation coefficient.

Statistics do not allow you to turn off your brain. Not all issues can be resolved by statistical procedures.

6

The Theory of Relativity

To keep things as concrete as possible, this chapter will be concerned primarily with the batting average. The principles and procedures, however, apply to any statistic. The batting average was selected as an example because of its familiarity.

An alphabetical listing of American League players in 1988 shows that Brook Jacoby had a batting average of .241. That means .241 hits per at-bat or that he hit safely on 24.1 percent of his at-bats or that he averaged one hit every 4.15 times at bat. These tidbits by themselves are not really very interesting unless you are a big Cleveland fan or Jacoby's agent. To put it in perspective, it is necessary to know how his batting average compares with those of other players in the league. To someone familiar with batting averages, a value of .241 indicates that he does not compare favorably, but just how unfavorably? Exactly how did Jacoby stand in relation to other batters in the league? Was he near the bottom or somewhere near the middle? To answer this question, it is necessary to consider Jacoby's average relative to those of other players.

The first step is to specify exactly what other players are to be used for comparison. Actually, Jacoby could be compared with any group of players imaginable, for whatever reason. Most often, a player's average is to be compared with those of all of the other players in the league for that season, but any set of players would be legitimate. His average could be compared with those of all other players at his position or the players on his team. His average in one season might even be compared with his average in all the other seasons he played. Whatever group is to be used, this group will be called the *reference group*.

In some cases, the player is a member of the reference group. When we compare Jacoby's 1988 batting average with those of other players in the 1988 season, Jacoby was part of that reference group and helped determine its performance. For other reference groups, he might not be a member. His performance could be compared, for example, with the 1927 American League players. But simpler cases first. Here are the batting averages for the 14 American League third basemen in 1988 who played the most games at that position. Jacoby is a member of that highly variable group.

Boggs	.366	Jacoby	.241
Brookens	.243	Lansford	.279
Buechele	.250	Lyons	.269
Gaetti	.301	Molitor	.312
Gonzales	.215	Pagliarulo	.216
Gruber	.278	Presley	.230
Howell	.254	Seitzer	.304

How does Jacoby's batting average compare with this group? There are several ways to answer this question: ranking, cumulative percentages, normalized averages, or standard scores.

Ranking

The simplest number that reflects a player's standing in the group is his *rank*. The procedure for ranking was encountered in Chapter 2. If we ranked the above values (place them in order), Jacoby would rank eleventh.

Cumulative Percentage

Knowing that Jacoby ranked eleventh among AL third basemen in batting average is of little value unless the number of third basemen is known. In this case, there is one for each team, but the size of many reference groups may not be as well known. It would not be very helpful to know that a player ranked 51 among all regular American League players unless the size of this reference group was known.

The problem becomes more significant when two players from different reference groups are being compared—for example, if Jacoby was being compared with some National League third baseman or a third baseman from 1941. A rank of 11 in the AL, where there are 14 teams, compared with a similar rank in the NL, where there are also 14 teams, would not be confusing, but in 1941 there were only 8 teams, so a rank of 11 is not possible. The solution is relatively simple. Just as dividing hits by at-bats compensates for differences in the latter, dividing the ranks by the total number of players will compensate for any differences in the size of the relative reference groups.

The ranking may be approached in either direction. It is possible to ask what proportion or percentage of players had a *lower* batting average than Jacoby, or conversely, what proportion or percentage of players had a *higher* batting average than Jacoby.

Of the 14 players, Jacoby ranked eleventh from the top. There were only 3 players below him. Dividing 3 by 14 and multiplying by 100 results in a value of 21.4. Therefore, 21.4 percent of the players had lower averages than Jacoby. Conversely, Jacoby's eleventh-place ranking means that ten players had higher batting averages than he did. Looking at it from this perspective, $10/14 \times 100 = 71.4$ percent of the players attained a higher average than he did. Either expression is a valid representation of Jacoby's relative standing in his group and is unconfounded by group size.*

Here are the percentages for each of the 14 players. The value given is the percentage of players that had a batting average *lower* than that player. In other words, 92.9 percent (13/14) of the players had a batting average lower than Wade Boggs's, 85.7 percent had a batting average lower than Paul Molitor's, and so on.

	H/AB	Rank	Cum %		H/AB	Rank	Cum %
Boggs	.366	1	92.9	Howell	.254	8	42.9
Molitor	.312	2	85.7	Buechele	.250	9	35.7
Seitzer	.304	3	78.6	Brookens	.243	10	28.6
Gaetti	.301	4	71.4	Jacoby	.241	11	21.4
Lansford	.279	5	64.3	Presley	.230	12	14.3
Gruber	.278	6	57.1	Pagliarulo	.216	13	7.1
Lyons	.269	7	50.0	Gonzales	.215	14	0.0

To compare Jacoby (or any other player) with a player who is not in this reference group, it is best to compute the cumulative percentage for the players being compared within their own reference groups and then compare the respective percentage values. Red Rolfe of the Yankees had a batting average of .264 in 1941. Although this is .023 higher than that Jacoby attained in 1988, the league as a whole had a much higher batting average in 1941. Of the eight American League third basemen in 1941, Rolfe ranked fifth in batting average. In terms of cumulative percentages, 37.5 percent of the 1941 third basemen had poorer batting averages than Rolfe. Thus, relative to their respective reference groups, Rolfe did outperform Jacoby, who beat out only 21.4 percent of the third basemen in his season.

It does not make statistical sense to "transport" Jacoby into the 1941

---

*A statistically more sophisticated approach to the problem would involve computing what are known as percentile ranks. The computations, however, are tedious, and for all practical purposes there is little to be gained by the increased effort. Most introductory texts on statistical analysis describe the computational procedure in detail.

sample and compute his rank or percentage rank. Therefore, questions such as "What would Jacoby's rank have been among 1941 third basemen?" admit of no sensible statistical answer.

Normalized Statistics

Knowing that Jacoby attained a higher average than 21.4 percent of the league's third basemen that season tells us more than just his rank but still is not the end of the story. The tenth player could have outhit him by .025 or .001, and he would still rank eleventh, and each of the players below him could have hit less than .150 without changing Jacoby's relative position or his percentage rank.

More information about Jacoby's performance in relation to the group would be available if his average could be compared to some value that would best indicate the performance of the entire group—the *overall* batting average, obtained by adding up the hits for all of the players and dividing that figure by their total number of at bats. The difference between Jacoby's batting average and that of the group would then indicate how he stood in relation to the group's overall performance.

The 1988 third basemen as a group had a combined batting average of .273. The absolute difference between Jacoby's average and those of all of the league's third basemen was thus −.032. In common parlance, he batted 32 points below the league average for third basemen. The difference may also be expressed as a percentage by dividing Jacoby's average by that of the group and multiplying by 100. Jacoby's relative performance would then be

$$RBA = (BA \text{ player} / BA \text{ group}) \times 100 = (.241 / .273) \times 100 = 88.3*$$

With this measure, a player whose average is the same as that of the reference group will score 100, and relative standing will be reflected by how far above or below 100 his value is. This measure has been called the *normalized batting average* by baseball analysts. The term *normalized* is technically incorrect since that term has a statistical meaning beyond that used here, but common custom dictates its use in this context.

For measures in which a high score indicates poor performance, such as earned run average, the numerator and denominator are interchanged. Normalized earned run average is

$$NERA = ERA \text{ group} / ERA \text{ player} \times 100$$

The effect of this transformation is to make values over 100 "good" values and values under 100 "bad" values.

The same procedure may be applied to comparisons from different reference groups. In 1941, the league third basemen had a combined batting average of .266. Rolfe's normalized batting average would be 99.3, which is still higher than Jacoby's 88.3.

Percentage rank and normalized batting average do not always lead to the same conclusion. Pete Suder, who was the Athletics third baseman in 1941, had a batting average of .245, which ranked him seventh, better than only 12.5 percent of the other third basemen and somewhat below Jacoby's 21.4 percent. Yet his normalized batting average was 92.1, which is a bit higher than Jacoby's. Comparison of normalized batting averages also will not necessarily agree with ones made on actual batting averages. For example, Steve Lyons of the White Sox had a batting average of .269 in 1988, as did Ken Keltner of Cleveland in 1941. Both had cumulative percentage scores of 50 percent among third basemen. Keltner, on the other hand, had a normalized batting average of 101.1, while Lyons's normalized batting average was 98.5.

This does not mean that one measure is better than the other or that some measures are providing false information. Statistics do not lie; only statisticians can do that. Different measures indicate different properties of the data. In comparing the batting averages of two players, the difference immediately indicates that one player performed differently than the other on that measure. When comparing the performance of players relative to the performance of other players who played under more or less the same conditions, the cumulative percentage indicates the relative *ranking* of the players within their reference group, and the absolute difference between the average and the reference group average or the normalized batting average provides the relative difference between the player's batting average and the overall average of the reference group. It all depends upon the kind of information desired.

Baseball analysts have generally adopted the normalized or proportional statistic for making these kinds of comparisons. Conclusions based on absolute or proportional differences can sometimes be quite different. A simple example will illustrate the problem.

	League Avg.	Player Avg.	Abs. Diff	Norm.
Foxx, 1930	.303	.335	.032	111
Horton, 1967	.249	.281	.032	113
Donaldson, 1967	.249	.276	.027	111

Which player performed relatively best? The absolute difference assumes that differences mean the same irrespective of their location. Foxx and Horton performed the same, each 32 points above the league average, and both were better than Donaldson. The normalized statistic assumes that differences among players are more "important" when the reference-group average is lower. In other words, a difference of .032 in the batting average of 1930 players who had an overall batting average of .303 is less important than the same difference for 1967 players whose overall average was only .249. Thus Horton performed relatively better than Foxx, whose performance is now the same as that of Donaldson. Choice of measures, and the arguments made from them, depend upon which assumption is most reasonable for the situation. There is no statistical reason to embrace one or the other.

When relative batting averages were originally proposed by David Shoebotham in 1976, the player's own record was not counted in computing the overall batting average when he was to be compared with other players in the same reference group. The logic was that it was somehow unfair to compare a player with himself. The practice does not seem justified on either practical or logical grounds. If the reference group is large, even removing the most extreme case does not change the overall average by a significant amount. For example, removing Boggs's league-leading average of .366 from the 1988 American League average of .259, which was based on over 75,000 at-bats, reduced the league batting average by only .00073. The removal of players whose averages are closer to the overall average would necessarily have less effect. Removing Jacoby's totals from the league totals left the league average in 1988 unchanged at .259.

For a small reference group (such as third basemen), the effect of removing one player may be considerable. However, the logic of normalizing averages rests on the comparison of a player's position with that of the reference group as a whole, not just the performance of his colleagues. The player's contribution to the group of which he is a member is as important to the group's overall performance as anyone else in that group and should be included. It is the group average that is providing the standard of comparison, not just other players'. Whether the player is part of that group is irrelevant. Moreover, eliminating the player gives an advantage to the better or the poorer player since removing his contribution will have a greater effect on the overall average than removing the contribution of a player near the average.

The choice of a *reference point* is always arbitrary, and a player may be compared with any reference point to fit the purpose. Relative averages have been computed using the largest or the smallest value as the reference as well as the league average. For example, Jacoby's average normalized to the largest average (Boggs's) would be $.241 / .366 \times 100 = 65.9$. There is nothing magic about any of these procedures. In interpreting the result of any statistical operation, the important thing is what those operations have done to the numbers as well as what the numbers represent.

Standard Scores

While the absolute difference and normalized batting average have the advantage of computational simplicity and are easily understood, they still miss the mark somewhat. The only quantity that contributes to the computation of the normalized batting average is the overall batting average. As long as the reference group's overall batting average was .259, Jacoby's normalized average would be 93.1, regardless of how the players above and below him performed.

Suppose Jacoby is compared with four other players who had a combined 2250 at-bats and 584 hits (batting average .260). Adding Jacoby's totals to these gives 2802 at-bats and 717 hits, for an average of .256. Now suppose the individual at-bats and hits of those four players were as follows:

	AB	H	BA
O'Brien	547	149	.272
Davis	600	161	.268
Guillen	566	148	.262
Jacoby	552	133	.241
White	537	126	.235
Total	2802	717	.256

The range of individual batting averages was from .235 to .272. Jacoby would rank fourth in this not so scintillating list at .241, with a normalized batting average of $(.241 / .256) \times 100 = 94.1$.

Now suppose that the four other players had these records:

	AB	H	BA
Henderson	507	154	.304
Gantner	539	149	.276
Sveum	467	113	.242
Jacoby	552	133	.241
Evans	437	91	.208
Total	2502	640	.256

Note that the group still has an overall average of .256, and as a member of this more variable group, Jacoby would still have a normalized batting average of 94.1 because the overall average of the five players has not changed. However, his average is *relatively* closer to the average of the group in the second set because the other players are spread out further than they were in the first group (ranging from .208 to .304). It is possible to compute a score for Jacoby (or any other player) that takes into account not only the overall average score but also the spread of those scores. In other words, if a player differs from the overall average by 20 points when most of the players are close to that average, his deviation means more than when all of the scores are well spread out.

The standard deviation, because it measures this spread and is in the same units as the original values, provides an ideal way to deal with this situation.

The procedure involves converting the statistic to a *standard score*. The standard score begins with the difference between a player's statistic, say the batting average, and the mean statistic of the reference group, then expresses that difference in terms of standard-deviation units.

A simple analogy will illustrate how a standard score is constructed. Suppose a stack of lumber of different lengths has a mean length of 60 inches. Suppose also that the board on the top of the stack is 36 inches long. The difference between this board and the mean is 24 inches. However, this difference can be expressed in feet by simply dividing the number of feet by the number of inches in a foot $(24/12 = 2)$. The board differs from the mean by 24 inches or 2 feet. Now suppose that the standard deviation is 6 inches. Since the standard deviation is in inches, the difference may be expressed in standard deviations by dividing the difference of 24 inches by 6. Therefore, the board deviates from the mean by $24/6$ or 4 standard deviations. If a foot is 12 inches, the board's length may be stated in feet. If a standard deviation is 6 inches, its length may be stated in standard deviations. It is merely a change in units. The board hasn't changed.

Likewise, the difference between a player's batting average and the mean batting average for a reference group can be expressed in batting-average units. The mean batting average of 14 third basemen was .268, and the standard deviation was .041. The difference between Jacoby's batting average and the mean is $.241 - .268 = -.027$ (always subtract the mean from the individual value, so that values less than the mean will be negative). If this difference is divided by the standard deviation, however, it is now in standard-deviation units. Jacoby's batting average expressed as a standard score then is $-.027/.041 = -.66$. Since the size of the standard deviation is based on how variable the values are, the standard score represents the difference between the individual value and the mean in relation to the variability of the values. A difference value expressed in standard-deviation units is called a *z-score*.

In the examples at the beginning of this section, the overall batting average of both reference groups was .256. Jacoby's .241 differed from the mean of each group by $-.015$ $(.241 - .256)$. In the first case, however, the standard deviation was only .015, so Jacoby's batting average was −1.00 standard deviations from the overall average. When the batting averages are more variable (SD = .033), a difference of −.015 does not mean as much, so now it is just −.46 standard deviations from the mean. In other words, relative to other players, Jacoby's .241 is considered closer to average when the other players differ more from the average.

The computation of standard scores requires both the mean and the standard deviation of the reference group. The mean is subtracted from each original value, and each difference is divided by the standard deviation. The ratio will be positive or negative depending upon whether the original value lies above or below the mean. The mean of a set of z-scores is always 0, and the standard deviation of the z-scores is always 1, regardless of the original values. Note that the reference point is the *mean* of the batting averages, not the overall batting average.

By multiplying each z-score by 10, then adding 100, z-scores are transposed to a scale where the mean is 100 and the standard deviation 10. This not only avoids the nuisance of negative values but also provides whole numbers. We have carried out the computation of z-scores and standardized them to a base of 100 for American League third basemen. The mean was obtained by summing the batting averages and dividing by 14 (mean = .268). The standard deviation of .041 was obtained using the procedure described in Chapter 2. The values of z result from dividing each of the difference values in the second column by .041:

	BA	BA-M	z	Standard
Boggs	.366	.098	2.39	123.9
Molitor	.312	.044	1.07	110.7
Seitzer	.304	.036	.88	108.8
Gaetti	.301	.033	.80	108.0
Lansford	.279	.011	.27	102.7
Gruber	.278	.010	.24	102.4
Lyons	.269	.001	.02	100.2
Howell	.254	−.014	−.34	96.6
Buechele	.250	−.018	−.44	95.6
Brookens	.243	−.025	−.61	93.9
Jacoby	.241	−.027	−.66	93.4
Presley	.230	−.038	−.94	90.6
Pagliarulo	.216	−.052	−1.26	87.4
´ Gonzales	.215	−.053	−1.29	87.1

Mean = .268

Standard Deviation = .041

The zero point and standard-deviation scale for converting z-scores to standard scores are completely arbitrary. They could be made to look more like batting averages if the mean was taken to be 250 and the standard deviation 30. Boggs would then have a standardized batting average of $250 + (2.39 \times 30) = 322$, and Gonzales a standardized batting average of $250 - (1.29 \times 30) = 211$. Jacoby's batting average standardized in this way would be $250 - (66 \times 30) = 230$.

The standard score uses the mean of the individual values as a reference point in all computations. To be meaningfully interpreted, the mean and standard deviation of the individual values must be an appropriate representation of the performance of the group. Sometimes, the mean is not a good representative value. If the mean was computed using every player in the American League, the mean batting average would be misleading since there are many players who have just a few at-bats, and each one would contribute as much to the group mean as the regular players who have hundreds of at-bats.

In most cases, where large numbers of players are involved and the number of at bats contributed by each player is relatively large, this is not a problem. Usually you are not interested in those players who do not play much. For example, in computing a "league mean" based only on players who have at least 200 at-bats (more or less), the mean and standard deviation will probably be fairly representative of the central tendency for that group. In any event, one should be careful in computing and interpreting standard scores. While it is not statistically incorrect to use standard scores regardless of what the mean and standard deviation may be, how they are interpreted may be affected by reference points (means and standard deviation) that are not representative of overall group performance.

Relative statistics are not necessary to make comparisons of players from different reference groups. It is just as true to state that Rolfe had a higher batting average in 1941 (.262) than Jacoby in 1988 (.241) as it is to state that his normalized average was 99.2, compared to Jacoby's 88.2, or that his standard score was 99.9, compared to Jacoby's 93.4. The theoretical assumption that has motivated the use of relative statistics is that differences in playing conditions that affect the entire league should be parsed out of a statistic. The interpretation of relative statistics, however, is not quite this uncomplicated. The problem will resurface in Chapter 9 after some other matters have been dealt with.

Batting Runs: A Special Case

This whole matter of relative statistics is irrelevant to batting runs. If the constant a (the multiplier of outs) is computed from a reference group to which the player belongs, the statistic is already expressed relative to the overall performance of that group, the number of runs above or below the average player. Since it is the number of runs, not the percentage, the difference is essentially an absolute difference (the score minus the league average) rather than a normalized statistic.

Without knowing the actual average, one cannot convert batting runs to a normalized measure, but it is possible to standardize batting runs for any group of players, just like any other statistic. It is conveniently true that the standard deviation of the absolute differences is the same as the standard deviation of the original scores. Therefore, if batting runs, which is already expressed as a difference value, is divided by the standard deviation of the reference group, it will produce a score in standard-deviation units. It is not a z-score, however, because batting runs is a deviation from the overall reference group value, not its mean.

Pitching Runs

In some baseball statistics compendia, a statistic called pitching runs is reported. This should not be confused with the pitching runs statistic that may be computed from a pitcher's LWTS. The pitching runs discussed by most baseball analysts is actually nothing more than a normalized earned run average.

7

Statistical Reliability:
The Standard Error

One bad hop, one bad call by an umpire, one windblown popfly, one fly ball lost in the sun, or one unfavorable decision by the official scorer may not seem like much, but when you realize that the difference between a .280 batting average and a .300 batting average is only two hits in 100 at-bats, such things may be of great concern.

Baseball statisticians are concerned with these effects because they know that the value of any statistic is affected by unsystematic factors; that is, things like the above that vary in a more or less unpredictable way from plate appearance to plate appearance. Players become very philosophical about these individual inequities because they have an implicit faith that given enough at-bats, the breaks will even out, and the statistic will truly reflect what they are capable of accomplishing. They and management know the problems involved in trying to evaluate a player's performance when the number of plate appearances is too small.

Any statistic is based on a specific sample of plate appearances or batters faced. Since the purpose of that statistic is to evaluate a player's performance on that set of at-bats, one of the first considerations must be the accuracy with which the statistic represents the status of the player on whatever quality the statistic is supposed to measure. If two players differ on that quality, the statistic must consistently differentiate between those players. This accuracy or consistency is known as *reliability* — in this sense, solely the ability of the statistic to separate one player from another. It has nothing to do with whether the statistic measures anything important.

Any statistic consists of two components that combine to determine its actual computed value: the true value and error. In equation form, where X is the obtained value of the statistic,

$$X = T + E$$

The error component is the combined effect of all of the unsystematic factors that affect the statistic. Since these effects are unsystematic and random, over a sufficient number of plate appearances their effect would balance out, and the obtained value of the statistic would equal the true value. Theoretically, however, it would take an infinite number of plate appearances for the errors perfectly to balance, so we never actually obtain the true value. Therefore, when we observe a difference between players on some statistic, some of that difference is due to real (systematic) differences and some to random error.

Factors contributing to T and factors contributing to E are defined solely in terms of their effect. The difference between two players that is attributable to T is the difference that would remain after an infinite number of plate appearances. That attributable to E would disappear. It is not just things like bad hops that are random. More interesting things, such as the difficulty of the pitches that the batter is required to hit, may also vary from plate appearance to plate appearance and over a long series of at-bats will behave as a random factor. All that is necessary is that it average out to be the same for all players.

A bit of simple algebra will provide a more technical meaning of reliability. For any group of players ranked on some statistic, we can compute the mean for that statistic. In terms of true and error components, the mean is

$$M(X) = M(T) + M(E)$$

Wherever there is a mean, there is also a variance (the square root of which is the standard deviation). Likewise, then, the following relation exists:

$$Var(X) = Var(T) + Var(E)$$

Since the variance measures the variability (the differences between players), reliability may then be defined as the proportion of true variance in the obtained value of a statistic. Mathematically, this is easily expressed

$$R = Var(T) / Var(X)$$

But since $Var(T) = Var(X) - Var(E)$, the reliability may be written as

$$R = 1 - Var(E) / Var(X)$$

If it is difficult to get an intuitive feel for what this means, think of the variance as a measure of the differences between players. When it is stated that some factor contributes a proportion of the variance, it means that it contributes that proportion to whatever it is that makes these players

different. Therefore, error variance represents that part of the differences between players that is due to unsystematic error; the rest is the true
variance—that contributed by any real difference between players.

If there were no error, a list of players ranked according to a particular
statistic would be determined only by the systematic factors that affected
their performance. However, if the error is large relative to differences in the
true score, the lists would be unstable because the ranking of players would
be dependent mostly on random factors. If we took another set of plate appearances, the list would look entirely different. To put any faith in the ranking of players on some particular statistic, it is necessary that the statistic
actually indicate differences among players on systematic factors and not
just error. A measure of reliability, therefore, tells us how much the
differences between players are to be trusted.

Computation of Reliability

From the formula for R, two quantities are necessary in order to compute the reliability. Var(X), the variance of the statistic in a group of players,
may be directly computed using the procedure described in Chapter 2. It is
simply the variance (SD^2) for the actual values. Error variance, however, cannot be directly obtained and must be estimated. For any additive statistic for
which a value is available on each plate appearance, at-bat, or batter faced,
a simple procedure may be used to obtain an estimate of Var(E). This includes the proportion in any single category as well as derived statistics such
as batting average, on-base average, slugging average, isolated power, and
in principle total offense and batting runs. It may also be used for simple proportions based on any other countable denominator, such as runs (or earned
runs) per plate appearance or batter faced, stealing success rate, or won-lost
percentage.

The computational example will be carried out for the batting averages
of five players. You will recall from Chapter 2 that three quantities are
necessary to obtain a sum of squares, and hence the variance: the sum of
the individual values, the sum of the squared values, and the number of
those values. If you think of the number assigned to each at-bat for each
player as either a 1 (hit) or 0 (out), then the sum of scores is simply the number of hits. The sum of the squared values is also equal to the number of hits,
since each squared value is also a 1 or 0. The number of values is equal to
the number of at-bats.

We begin by computing the overall mean of hits for all players by
dividing the total number of hits by the total number of at-bats. The result
is the overall batting average. Next we can subtract that mean from the value

on each at-bat for each player (either 1 or 0) to produce a deviation value for that at-bat. The sum of the squares of those deviations (SStot) divided by the number of at-bats would be the variance of those values (total variance).

Each of these differences, however, consists of two parts. One part is the difference between the original value (X = 1 or 0) and Mp, the mean for the player from which the score came (X – Mp). The other is the difference between the player's mean and the overall mean for all players (Mp – M). In equation form,

$$X - M = (X - Mp) + (Mp - M)$$

The relation is shown graphically in this figure.

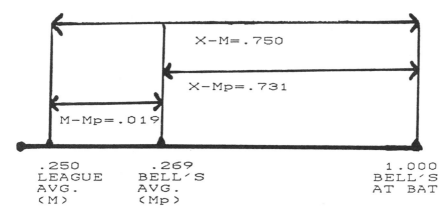

Example: Suppose the mean league batting average is .250. George Bell has a batting average of .269. On his first at-bat, Bell had a hit. The deviation from the league average for that at-bat would be 1 – .250 = .750. This consists of two parts: 1 – .269 = .731, which is the difference between the value for that at-bat from Bell's average, and .269 – .250 = .019, the deviation of Bell's average from the league average. In other words, the sum of the two components (.731 + .019) is .750, the total deviation for that at-bat.

If one computed the variance based on the first component, (X – Mp), it would reflect the variability *within* the player's at-bats—how much the result of each at-bat varies on the average from the overall mean of *his* at-bats. The variance based on the second component reflects the variability from player to player; that is, how much the average of that player's at-bats differs from those of other players. The variance within a player's at-bats is due to unsystematic errors, Var(E), because unsystematic error varies from at-bat to at-bat. The variability between players is due to differences in obtained value of the statistic Var(X). Therefore, 1 minus the ratio of the two variances would be equal to the reliability.

As in Chapter 2, the variance may be computed directly by computing the sum of squares from the sum and the sum of squared values rather than by computing each difference score. In practice, it is also easier to compute the sum of squares based on differences between the individual values and the overall mean, $X - M$, for all players (SS-Total) and the sum of squares based on differences between players, $MP - M$ (SS-Players), then obtain SS-error by subtracting the latter from the former.

Here is the complete computation:

	Boggs	Henderson	Bell	Clark	Ripken	Total
AB	584	507	614	496	512	2713
H	214	154	165	120	106	759
1	1	0	1	1	0	
2	0	1	0	0	0	
3	0	0	1	0	0	
4	1	0	0	0	1	
•	•	•	•	•	•	
•	•	•	•	•	•	
•	•	•	•	•	•	
a. Sum	214	154	165	120	106	759
b. Squares	214	154	165	120	106	759

Corrector $(C) = 759^2 / 2713 = 212.34$

SS (Tot) $= (759 - 212.34) = 546.66$
SS (Players) $= 214^2 / 584 + 154^2 / 507 \ldots + 106^2 / 512 - 212.34 =$
    $78.42 + 46.78 + 44.34 + 29.03 + 21.95 - 212.34 = 8.18$
SS (error) $= 546.66 - 8.18 = 538.48$

Var(X) $= 8.18 /$ No. of Players minus $1 = 8.18 / 4 = 2.05$
Var(E) $= 538.48 /$ Total AB $-$ No. of Players $= 2713 - 5 = 538.48 / 2708 = .199$

$R = 1 - .199 / 2.05 = 1 - .097 = .903$

Let us follow this example through in some detail. In computing a sum of squares from the sums and summed squares, you must subtract a value that consists of the square of the sum of all values, divided by the total number of values. This subtraction factor, or corrector (C), will be used repeatedly, so it may be computed first. The next step is to compute the sum of squared deviations of the individual values from the overall mean (SS-total) by totaling all the squared values (the sum of the five values in row b [squares]) and subtracting C.

The sum of squares for the difference between players is a bit more complicated. To obtain this sum of squares, we first square the total hits (sum of the 1s) for each player, divide each of these squares by the number of at-bats, sum the results for all players, and subtract C. Because the two component sums of squares must add up to the total, the sum of squares for error is simply equal to the sum of squares total minus the sum of squares between players.

The variance is defined as the mean of the sum of squares. For statistical reasons that need not concern us here, each sum of squares is divided by the number of values *minus 1* rather than just the number of values. The two variances you need are based on SS(Players) and SS(E). The number of players is 5; therefore, the variance for players (Var[X]) is SS(Players) / 4. The appropriate divisor for SS (error) is equal to the total number of at-bats less one for each player: $2713 - 5 = 2708$. That is, Var(E) = SS (Error) / 2708.

Having obtained Var(X) and Var(E), the reliability (R) is computed as shown. Essentially, a reliability of .903 means that 90 percent of the differences between these five players may be attributed to systematic factors. The rest is error.

The computation of R for any simple proportion or any unweighted sum (e.g., on-base average) may be carried out in identical fashion. For on-base average, a player receives a 1 on a plate appearance that results in any hit, base on balls, or being hit by the pitcher and a 0 otherwise.

When the various components are weighted differently (as in slugging average or isolated power), the sums and sums of squared values for a player are computed somewhat differently. For slugging average, a player receives a value of 1 for a single, 2 for a double, 3 for a triple, and 4 for a home run, and 0 for any other outcome. The sum for each player (row a) is therefore his total bases (the sum of $1B \times 1$, $2B \times 2$, $3B \times 3$, and $HRs \times 4$). The sum of squared values (row b) would be the number of times each event occurred times the square of the bases gained on that event ($1B \times 1$, $2B \times 4$, $3B \times 9$, $HR \times 16$). The same principle applies in computing the totals for isolated power, except that the weights are 0 for an out or single, 1 for a double, 2 for a triple, and 3 for a home run. Once the values for rows a and b are obtained, the computation of R is carried out in the same way. A complete computational example for the slugging average (weighted frequencies) is provided in Appendix B.

In computing the sums and squares for total offense and batting runs, one can follow the same principle. For total offense, each plate appearance receives the same values as for slugging average, except that a base on balls or being hit by the pitcher receives a value of 1. For batting runs, each single receives a value of .46, each double a value of .80, and so on. The sum (row a) is therefore equal to total batting runs, and the squares (row b) are equal to the frequency of each event multiplied by the *square* of the weight (e.g. $[.46^2 \times 16] + [.8^2 \times 2b] \ldots + [a^2 \times outs]$).

A vexing problem occurs when the results of attempted steals are included in total offense and batting runs. To compute the squares for each player (row b), it is necessary to know the value obtained on each plate appearance. In the computation of both total offense and batting runs, a successful steal adds to the weighted value of the event (+1 for total offense, .30 for batting runs), and being caught stealing subtracts from that total (−1 for total offense, −.60 for batting runs).

The problem arises because it is generally not known what event preceded a particular attempted stolen base (single, double, etc.), so it is not possible to determine the value for that plate appearance. In principle, exact values for each plate appearance on which a steal is attempted can be obtained. However, they require play-by-play data for each player.

To obtain a measure of reliability for total offense or batting runs, it is usually necessary to eliminate the results of attempted steals from the total or make some assumptions about when those steals took place. Since for most players steal attempts do not occur on a very large proportion of plate appearances, omitting them from the computation of reliability is not likely to have a large effect on the overall value of R. The exception is a set of players that contains a large number of players who steal frequently.

The other procedure is to estimate the events on which attempts occurred and adjust the values for individual plate appearances accordingly. The result has no effect on the sum (row a), but the particular assumptions will have an effect on the squares (row b). The magnitude of this effect will depend on how many attempts are involved and how much the assumed results deviate from reality.*

The reliability of some statistics (runs created, production index) cannot be determined in this way because they are not additive over individual at-bats, plate appearances, or any other unit in the denominator. This restriction also includes statistics based on outs (total average, earned run average) because a particular event (hit, out, single, home run, earned run, etc.) cannot be identified with a particular out. The reason is the same in both cases. Obtaining a sum of squares requires that you square the value of the numerator for each instance. Individual values do not exist for nonadditive statistics.

Reliability computed in this way should not be considered a universal

---

*It is a curious inconsistency that both total offense and batting runs treat the effect of an attempted steal identically, regardless of the circumstances. For example, the consequences of an attempted steal of third are certainly different from those of an attempted steal of second. In the case of total offense, for example, any steal adds 1 to bases gained, but an out at second "erases" a 1, while an out at third might erase a 2 if second base was gained on a double. For batting runs, the situation is incredibly complex, and to remain consistent with the philosophy of batting runs, it would be necessary to consider the run-producing potential of various events followed by a steal or being caught stealing. Certainly, a steal of second does not produce the same run potential as a steal of third.

quality of the statistic that is independent of the players and the conditions under which it is obtained. There is no single reliability for *the* batting average. It tells you about the particular set of values upon which it was computed.

Since reliability is the ratio of error variance to systematic variance, it will change with an increase or decrease in the contribution of either component. For a constant level of error variance, the reliability will be low if the players do not differ much from one another. Conversely, large differences between players will insure high reliability.

Reliability also depends upon the number of plate appearances, at-bats, or batters faced. Error variance will be larger with small numbers of plate appearances because differences will not randomize out as well. With a larger number of plate appearances, error variance contributes a smaller proportion of a given difference between players.

Reliability (R) is not a correlation coefficient. It does have a limiting value of +1 when the proportion of unsystematic error becomes very small with respect to the true variance, but negative values may be obtained that are less than –1.00, particularly when the differences between players is very low or the number of players being considered is small. Random variation, because it is random, may occasionally produce less variation in the values of the statistic than should be present. Negative reliability has no conceptual meaning, and negative values of R will occur primarily when there is nothing but random variation in a statistic—that is, whenever there is no real difference between players.

Every statistic is made up of some combination of frequencies from the batting, pitching, or fielding line, and it is the reliabilities of these individual proportions that actually determine the reliability of the overall statistic. The statistic itself affects reliability directly only in the way it weights its components. Heavy weighting of a highly reliable component will increase reliability, while weighting one of low reliability will decrease it.

For example, on-base average will usually have a higher reliability than batting average for any set of players. This is due to the inclusion of bases on balls, which is usually a highly reliable component, in the former. Likewise, most statistics that differentially weight home runs have higher reliability than batting average because home runs not only have high reliability, but weighting them increases their contribution to the total statistic. It is also likely that estimates of the reliability of total offense and batting runs will be slightly lower without including attempted steals than they would be if these data could be included because stolen bases is a highly reliable category.

Finally, the reliability of a compound statistic will increase if a highly correlated factor is added and decrease if a negatively correlated factor is added. These principles operate by increasing or decreasing differences between players (Var X), as indicated in Chapter 5.

Although high reliability is an admirable state, it is not nirvana. Weighting a category or otherwise adjusting a statistic just to improve reliability is not a realistic goal. For example, the reliability of batting runs may be improved by weighting outs +.50 instead of −.25. This makes no sense, however, because logically outs must have a negative weight.

The Standard Error and Confidence Intervals

Given an estimate of error variance, it is possible to compute a value called the *standard error*. The standard error of a statistic provides an estimate of the expected variation in that statistic for a single player in repeated sets of at-bats or plate appearances (e.g., from one season to another). In other words, it indicates how stable the value is for that player.

The standard error is defined as the square root of the ratio of error variance to plate appearances.

$$SE = SQRT \ (Var[E] / PA)$$

The error variance used in computing R is the pooled (average) error variance for all players in the list. The standard error refers to a single player and is quite sensitive to the number of plate appearances. Although it is more accurate to compute the standard error for each player, the pooled estimate is satisfactory unless the number of plate appearances or at-bats varies considerably from player to player. In the example, the standard error based on the pooled Var(E) would be

$$SE = SQRT \ (.199 / (2713 / 5) = .019^*$$

The standard error tells you how much you can expect a sample statistic to vary from the "true" value of the statistic. If the standard error was 0, the sample value would be equal to the true value. The mathematical properties of the standard error, however, are much more precise than that. The standard error is in the same units as the original statistic. An obtained value for any statistic will differ from the true value by more than one standard error

---

*For any simple proportion or unweighted sum of proportions, the error variance is equal to the product of the proportion of hits and the proportion of outs. The standard error is then obtained by dividing by the number of at-bats, plate appearances, or batters faced, and taking the square root. This simplifies the computation of the standard error in those cases considerably. The standard error for Boggs's batting average is SQRT ([.366 × .634] / 584) = .020.

less than one-third of the time. For our example, a player with about 550 at-bats would have a batting average that differed from the true value by more than .019 less than ⅓ of the time. Likewise, values that are more than 2 (actually 1.96) standard errors (.038) from the true value will be obtained less than 5 percent of the time.

The inverse is also true. The true value will not be more than 1.96 standard errors away from the obtained value more than 5 percent of the time. To rephrase this principle slightly, the true value must lie within 1.96 standard errors of the obtained value 95 percent of the time.*

This fact makes it possible to estimate the location of the true value as lying within a range of values called the *confidence limits.* If 95 percent of the time the obtained value will not deviate by more than 1.96 × the standard error from the true value, then 95 percent of the time the true value will be between $+(1.96 \times .019) = .037$ and $-(1.96 \times .019) = -.037$ of the sample value. If it is assumed that the true value lies between those points, there is a 95 percent chance of being correct. A player with an obtained batting average of .260 therefore should have a true value somewhere between .297 and .223. This interval is called the *95 percent confidence interval* because we are 95 percent sure that the true value is in that interval.

This seems terribly imprecise, and most people are surprised that the error in batting averages is that large. However, the confidence *level* of 95 percent is more or less arbitrary. There are no rules for deciding on a particular confidence level. The value of 95 percent is one that is commonly used in many fields in which true values are to be estimated from samples, but one could just as well choose some other level.

If more certainty is desired, the 1 percent level might be more appropriate. However, that would result in a larger range. The factor for 1 percent is 2.58 × the standard error, and the confidence interval for our .260 hitter would be between .309 and .211. Likewise, it is possible to restrict the range by decreasing the level of confidence. To be 80 percent certain, for example, the confidence limits would be from $+(1.28 \times .019)$ to $-(1.28 \times .019)$, or between .284 and .236. The range may be as small as one likes, but it must be paid for in the coin of less certainty (confidence) about its correctness. Precision is gained at the expense of accuracy.

Where did these criterion values of 1.28, 1.96, and 2.58 come from? To get into this problem would take us in even deeper than we are now. Let

---

This is the same principle used by public opinion polls to report how accurately their sample reflects true public opinion. They will say something like "The figure is accurate within 3 percent, 95 percent of the time." The 3 percent represents 1.96 × the standard error of their data. To translate this to baseball statistics, one would say that the batting average is accurate within 37 points 95 percent of the time. It doesn't sound very accurate, does it? Does it make you feel better about the whole thing to realize that the 95 percent confidence interval for career batting averages based on 5000 at-bats is about 10 points (.010)?

us simply say that they are based on the mathematical laws of probability. Mathematically, it is frequently true that unsystematic variation will produce sample statistics that deviate from the true value by more than $1.28 \times$ the standard error less than 20 percent of the time, more than $1.96 \times$ the standard error less than 5 percent of the time, and more than $2.58 \times$ the standard error less than 1 percent of the time. We will have occasion to use these criterion values, which we will call Z, in future discussions. A table of some convenient values of Z and their associated percentages is given in Appendix C, Table 1.

The same procedure and the same critical values will apply for any statistic for which the standard error is known and the number of plate appearances or at-bats is over 60. When the number of at-bats is less than 60, the equivalent criterion values are somewhat larger, and the table is not appropriate. Otherwise, for any given level of confidence,

$$\text{Upper Limit} = \text{Sample Mean} \times (Z \times SE)$$
$$\text{Lower Limit} = \text{Sample Mean} - (Z \times SE)$$

The size of the standard error and hence the size of the confidence interval are related to the size of the sample. Even casual fans understand that statistics are more stable the larger the number of plate appearances. The reliability coefficient and standard error verify this intuition. The true value of a statistic is never known. The larger a sample becomes, the closer the sample statistic is to the true value. If you have enough plate appearances, the standard error would eventually become negligible but will never be truly zero. It would require over 100,000 plate appearances to reduce the standard error for batting average below .001.

The Truth About the True Value

Do not fall into the trap of thinking of the portion of variance due to systematic variance as differences in the ability of players. Even in the absence of differences in error variance, there are a variety of factors that can produce systematic differences in performance between players. Many of these have little to do with the player. Remember that to qualify as a source of systematic variance, a factor has to be something that differs from player to player and will not randomize out over a large number of plate appearances. Differences in playing conditions, pitchers faced, injuries, and so on, are but some of the possible nonrandom factors that have little to do with ability or even motivation.

Depending on the situation, a particular factor may sometimes be systematic and sometimes unsystematic. For example, a player plays half of his games on his home field. In a sample of plate appearances taken from home games, the ballpark is a systematic effect for each player. In a group of players from different teams, their "true" scores will vary not only according to their ability but according to the effect of the field. In a sample of plate appearances taken from road games, however, the park effect is to some extent randomized since the plate appearances are distributed among almost all parks. The net result is a smaller relative contribution of park differences in statistics obtained from road games.

The main point, however, is that the "true" value of the statistic is a net result of all of the systematic effects. Those effects result from *anything* that makes the players differ from one another. We will consider this problem again in Chapter 10.

8

Differences Between Players

Unsystematic error is inescapable whenever a list of players is constructed on any measure. Even though the reliability of a list may be measured, there is little that can be done about it if reliability is not sufficiently high to permit adequate discrimination between players. If a certain player had 25 batting runs and another player had 22, there is little to choose between these players if the standard error is 10. Of course, any list of players constructed on a particular statistic is a bona fide list. That is indeed how they ranked on that statistic. But if the ranking is mostly a result of error variance, it makes little sense to argue about the relative merits of one player over another or use that list to predict future performance.

Suppose we have a list of players ranked on some statistic. We know that because of unsystematic error some of the differences between players are likely to be due to "chance." Which differences are likely to be due to real differences and which due to chance? Now, obviously those players further apart on the list stand a better chance of being really different than players that are close together. It would help our attempt to differentiate between players if we knew just how far apart they must be before a difference is meaningful.

There is no completely satisfactory answer to this question. In the final analysis, it boils down to what we believe. The situation is somewhat like a jury trial. The defendant is either guilty or not. The jurors make a decision based on what they consider evidence. The system is such that they are supposed to have evidence of guilt before they abandon the presumption of innocence. We are in much the same position. We begin by assuming that two players do not differ and require evidence that this is not the case. The more unreliable the measure, the tougher it is to obtain that evidence.

Moreover, just like a jury, we can be wrong. The jury tries not to convict an innocent person. We try not to assume that two players are different when they are not. When this happens, we say we have a *false positive*. Statistical analysis will allow us to determine how many false positives will occur but unfortunately will not identify them.

The first step is to compute a value called the *standard error of the difference*. Simply double Var(E), divide by the average number of at-bats, and take the square root.

$$SEd = SQRT \ (2 \times Var[E]) \ / \ avg. \ AB)$$

The standard error of the difference between two values is just like the standard error for a single value. Random error will produce *differences* between players larger than 1.96 standard errors of the difference less than 5 percent of the time by chance. Therefore, if we multiply the SEd by 1.96, the result is a *critical difference* (CD). Any difference larger than the critical difference will occur less than 5 percent of the time by chance. Statisticians call this a *significant difference*. Significance in this case has nothing to do with importance. It means *reliable* or not likely to be due to chance.

For our example based on five players, Var(E) for batting average was .199. Therefore,

$$SEd = SQRT \ ([2 \times .199] \ / \ 543) = SQRT \ (.00073) = .027$$

and the critical difference is

$$CD = 1.96 \times .027 = .053$$

In other words, given the error variance in this group of players, differences larger than .053 will occur less than 5 percent of the time by chance. That does not mean that 5 percent of the differences larger than .053 are false positives but that among any group of players who are not really different, 5 percent of them will differ by more than .053 from some players. Some differences are "real," however. That is why the procedure is unsatisfactory. We know only that some of the players who differ by more than .053 will be false positives, but we do not know which ones or even in any given group of players how many there are.

It does not appear that we have gained very much. After all, if we assumed the existence of random variation, we already suspected that some differences were due to chance. Actually, we have learned something about the players in the list, although it is not as specific as we would like. This can be seen graphically by listing the players in order horizontally, then underlining those players whose batting averages fall withing the CD of one another.

Boggs	Henderson	Bell	Clark	Ripken
.366	.304	.269	.242	.207

In the sample of players, Boggs is in a class by himself, but other than that, no two adjacent players differ from each other. Of course, there is a 5 percent chance that any given significant difference is not real.

We have also gained control over the number of false positives by setting the percentage where we want it to be. If you want virtually to eliminate false positives, you can set the criterion very high. If you use 3.00 instead of 1.96 as a multiplier in obtaining CD, there would be almost no false positives. The problem, of course, is that CD gets larger and larger. With a value of $Z = 2.58$, it is .070. With a value of 3, it is .081. Even keeping false positives at a modest 5 percent (1 in 20), two players are considered different only if their batting averages are separated by more than 50 points. If this seems like a stringent criterion, remember that 50 points is only 5 hits in 100 at-bats, which is not much of a difference. Major league baseball players are a fairly homogeneous lot. They are the 700 or so best players in the world. If you played games with a random sample of the world's population, batting averages over 550 at-bats would not all fall in the range from .200 to .350 as do those of major-leaguers.*

We can protect ourselves against false positives by setting the criterion high enough to keep them at a low rate. But in so doing, we may be defeating the whole purpose of our analysis. The purpose in the first place was to find out which players differ. In the way of the jury trial, we want to do more than protect the innocent—we want to convict the guilty. Unfortunately, there is something of an inverse relationship between the two goals. We can reduce the number of false positives (innocent people who are convicted) to any level we want, but in so doing we fail to find differences that really exist (set the guilty free as well). Statistical procedures, like justice systems, must compromise between these two.

We now turn to this opposite side of the coin. Suppose we set our false positive rate at 5 percent. How successful are we in finding differences that really exist? The answer depends on how big the difference really is. It stands to reason that given a fixed amount of random error, the obtained difference between two players is more likely to overshadow the effects of random error if the true difference between the players is large.

There are two ways of looking at this question. One is to fix the "success rate," say at 95 percent. We may then determine how large a true difference between two players must be before we will find 95 percent of those differences, still keeping the false positive rate at 5 percent. The procedure is to compute the *true difference* (TD). This value is equal to Z for the false

---

*High school, university, and youth baseball players undoubtedly differ more from one another in ability than major league players. This can be seen easily in the fact that the range of batting averages is much greater in these groups. This is why scouts seldom consider a player a genuine prospect unless his numbers are exceptionally good, considerably above the CD. Essentially, they are trying to produce a false positive rate near zero.

positive rate (Z_{fp}) minus Z for the success rate (Z_s) × SEd. From Table 1 in Appendix C, we see that Z for 5 percent is 1.96 and Z for 95 percent is −1.96. Therefore,

$$TD = (1.96 - [-1.96]) \times .027 = 3.92 \times .027 = .106$$

Whenever the success rate is 1 − false positive rate, TD will be double the CD. The exact meaning of TD is a bit complicated. If two players "really" differ by TD, the *obtained* difference will be greater than the CD 95 percent of the time. For our example, players who differ from each other by more than .106 will produce a value of CD greater than .053 95 percent of the time. Therefore, if two players differ by more than .106, you have a 95 percent chance of finding that difference. If they differ by less than .106, you have less than a 95 percent chance of finding it.

The choice of error and success rates is up to you because they essentially reflect how willing you are to entertain false beliefs with respect to who is different and who is not (convict the innocent and free the guilty).

The other way to look at the problem is to select the size of the difference you wish to be concerned with, then compute your success rate. The size of the difference is usually based on how important that difference is. In batting average, a 10-point (.010) difference is 1 hit in 100 at-bats. It could be argued that a difference that small is inconsequential. Suppose you decide, for whatever reason, that differences of .020 are important enough to be considered. How successful will you be in finding players who differ by at least that much when the false positive rate is 5 percent (CD = .053)? You need to find Z_s, then look up the percentage value in Table 1 that corresponds to it. This is obtained by subtracting the ratio of the difference to SEd from Z_{fp}, which for 5 percent is 1.96:

$$Z = 1.96 - (.020 / .027) = 1.96 - .74 = 1.22$$

Z is evaluated by comparing it with the values in Table 1. The success rate for our example is between 20 and 25 percent. The sad thing is that given the error variance for a particular statistic, if you are unhappy with the CD and your success rate, there is little that can be done about it. Statistics will tell you how you are doing but cannot change the situation to improve your odds. If the success rate and false positive rate are fixed, there is only one way to reduce the CD and TD: more at-bats or plate appearances. The error variance, Var(E), does not change as the number of at-bats increases, but SE and therefore SEd will decrease. Therefore, both CD and TD will decrease as the number of at-bats increases. That makes it possible to set a value for TD, a success rate, and a false positive rate, and compute how many at-bats are necessary to achieve that combination. First divide TD by the Z for false positive rate minus the Z for success rate. Then divide 2 times Var(E) by that quantity.

$$A = TD / (Z_{fp} - Z_{sr})$$
$$AB = 2 \times Var(E) / A^2$$

If we want TD = .020 (we want to find differences of over .020) with a success rate of 95 percent but to protect ourselves against false positives 95 percent of the time, we would need

$$A = .020 / (1.96 - (-1.96) = .020 / 3.92 = .0051$$
$$AB = (2 \times .199) / .0051^2 = .398 / .000026 = 15,308 \text{ at-bats.}$$

Sometimes what you want is not attainable. Remember, however, that the choice of false positive and success rates is up for grabs. If you are willing to accept higher error rates, a reasonable strategy may be within reach. One point cannot be made too often: Statistics do not provide answers or make decisions. They simply provide evidence. Often you can specify the consequences for making certain decisions, but when you reach the bottom line, the decision or the answer is up to you.

Identifying Excellence

In evaluating player performance, one of the most common problems is assessing special performance. For example, in the 1954 World Series, New York Giant outfielder Dusty Rhodes had 4 hits in 6 at-bats. This was hailed as a tremendous clutch performance. There have been other gems that caught people's eye. For example, Reggie Jackson was called "Mr. October" on the basis of a single World Series performance in which he had 7 hits in 11 at-bats and 5 home runs in the last three games. Many players appear to have a "career season" in which their performance surpasses their usual level, and others have "off years" in which they struggle to attain mediocrity. The League Championship Series and World Series, with intense media focus, often feature players who seem to "rise to the occasion" or "choke under pressure." It is a serious question, however, how much random variation contributes to this variability in performance and how much is actually due to the circumstances of the moment.

The standard error seems to offer a way to evaluate these situations. The logic is impeccable. Sample values that deviate more than 1.96 standard errors from the true value will occur less than 5 percent of the time. If a player's career statistic is assumed to be close to the true value and his performance in a particular year or series exceeds this value by more than 1.96 standard errors, it is unlikely to have happened by chance (unsystematic variation). Or so it seems.

Roberto Clemente had such a year. In 1967, he had a batting average of .357, which was 40 points above his career average of .317. Based on the sample of 585 at-bats that composed his 1967 sample, the standard error was .020. Therefore, Clemente's batting average in 1967 exceeded his expected average by .040 / .020, or 2.00 standard errors. Since a difference that large will occur less than 5 percent of the time by chance, it is tempting to conclude that this was not a chance deviation from .317 but occurred for some special reason.

The entire force of the conclusion depends on the proposition that one has uncovered an event unlikely to have occurred by chance. Statistics are ill equipped to deal with single events because they are more concerned with long-run occurrences. The *Baseball Encyclopedia* contains about 45,000 batting lines. Suppose for each player each of his season batting averages differed from his career average only by chance.* There would then be 5 percent, or about 2250 batting averages, in which the discrepancy from career average was larger than 1.96 standard errors.

How likely is it that Clemente's 1967 average is one of those? If a particular player and year were selected at random from the 45,000 entries, the likelihood would be .05, or 1 in 20, that it would deviate by more than 1.96 standard errors from the career average. But if Clemente's 1967 season was chosen *because* it appeared to deviate by a large amount, the odds of obtaining one of those 2250 instances would be much greater. You should not be surprised to find unlikely events if you look for them.

This means that comparisons using the standard error are rarely appropriate for answering questions about extreme performance by individual players in specific situations. Even if one searched the entire encyclopedia and found that 5000 instead of the expected 2250 entries had values more than 1.96 standard errors from the player's career average, one could not identify which were chance deviations and which genuine. There would even be some random variation in the actual number of special cases (as much as 225 in either direction one-third of the time), so that even if one found 2500 or so outstanding performances, one still would not know whether *any* of them were above chance.

The logic of probabilities requires that any sample be selected independent of actual performance. Then the long-run probabilities will apply. It is true, regardless of how you select a particular example, that 5 percent of the total possible cases will deviate by more than 1.96 standard errors from the

---

*This is somewhat oversimplified. Bill James suggests that a player's performance is usually somewhat lower at the beginning and end of his career than in the middle.

assumed true value, but the likelihood of actually obtaining one of those cases is only .05 if a case is chosen at random. In evaluating a player's performance in a particular set of at-bats, these conditions are seldom met because the question for a randomly selected batting line would not be very interesting.*

To compound the problem, there is an opposite side of the coin. Even if it were found that a particular performance did not exceed chance expectations, this is no guarantee that the player was not doing something special. Clemente should have reached the lofty heights of .357 only 5 percent of the time by chance with a true batting average of .317. But what if he had a special year in which his true average was .327? With a 5 percent criterion, he would have had to bat .357 before we would conclude that he deviated significantly from his normal performance. Yet even with a true batting average 10 points higher than usual, an average of .357 or more would occur only 7 percent of the time by chance.† The simple truth is that we cannot learn much about a specific player's unusual season or series performances from his statistics.

Regression

If one peruses the *Baseball Encyclopedia,* it soon becomes apparent that for almost every statistical category, whenever a player led the league in that category one year, he performed more poorly on that statistic the following year. In 1954, Willie Mays, then of the New York Giants, led the National League in batting average with .345. The following year his average was .317. In that same season, Dave Williams, also a Giant, had the lowest batting average in the league, .222. The following year it was .251.

This phenomenon is called *regression toward the mean.* It does not indicate that the good players are getting worse and the bad players better and in fact usually has nothing to do with changing ability. It is simply a statistical

---

*There is another way of approaching this problem. Take Clemente's case as an example. Clemente had 9454 at-bats. There are x number of samples of 585 consecutive at-bats that could be concocted out of this total. In how many of those samples will the batting average be .357 or higher? The answer is 5 percent, but the real problem is to determine the likelihood of finding at least one difference of that size in x such samples. This is similar to determining the chances of finding at least one difference that exceeds the CD in a set of x possible comparisons.

†If Clemente had an exceptional year in which his "true" batting average was .327, there is 1 chance in 20 that he would bat 40 points below that level—.287. Random variation can therefore create the paradox where a player is actually playing better but performing more poorly.

result of random variability.* Given his career average of .317, the probability that Clemente will have a batting average of .357 or higher is .05. If he achieves this level by chance, it means that next season, if nothing changes, the probability of equaling or exceeding .357 is still .05 and the probability that his batting average will be below .357 is .95. This does not mean that the true batting average has changed or that somehow the player has used up his allotment of hits by getting them all in one year but is more akin to "nowhere to go but down." After a run of 10 straight heads, the probability of a head on the next coin toss is still .50. To believe otherwise is "the gambler's fallacy."† Averages do not drop because they have to "catch up," only because chance events eventually even out.

Regression is a common phenomenon when dealing with successive samples. It may occur for teams as well. Statistically, the probability of an average team (.500) winning the next 10 games stays the same regardless of whether the team has just won 10 games, lost 10 games, or split 10 games. Yet a team that has won 10 in a row will inevitably not win another 10 in a row because 10 in a row is a rare event for an average team (1/1024).

Regression also causes serious practical problems. A player who was signed as a free agent after a career year will invariably do more poorly the succeeding year. It has nothing to do with his motivation or ability or his newfound wealth but is an inevitable result of the fact that the previous year was something of a statistical anomaly.§

Basically, the best prediction for any future performance is that it will be equal to the average of all previous performances.

**Regression to the mean was first discovered by an English scientist, Francis Galton, in 1885. Baseball statisticians have recently rediscovered it. They call it the up-down effect. Regression effects occur in many guises. This is only one of them. For example, a replacement manager more often that not performs better than his predecessor, at least for a while. Since managers are replaced when teams are faring poorly both by ability and by chance, this is more likely to be regression than managerial skill.*

†*It is a gross error to say that a player is "due" to get a hit because he has a string of hitless at-bats. The probability of a hit on any at-bat may change, but it does not necessarily increase as the number of hitless at-bats increases. That too is a manifestation of the gambler's fallacy.*

§*Questions of "momentum" and "struggling" are also relevant here. The emotional state correlated with success and failure should not be confused with the causal sequence of events. Whether momentum and over- and underachieving occur are complicated questions in which the role of regression should be considered.*

9

Validity

The ultimate test of any statistic is its *validity*. Most statistics are not haphazard combinations of categories but are designed with some purpose in mind. The classical definition of *validity* is the extent to which a statistic measures what it is intended to measure. Does it serve its purpose?

A statistic is not simply valid or nonvalid. Validity is always relative to some purpose. A statistic may be valid for one purpose but not for another. For example, the ubiquitous but occasionally maligned batting average may not be a valid measure of a player's ability to produce runs but may be a valid measure of his tendency to avoid making outs.

Any discussion of the validity of a statistic must therefore carefully define the *purpose* of the statistic—what it is valid for. *Purpose,* however, is another vague term with so many meanings that it renders most discussions of validity confusing. Just what is a statistic *for*? To some, the purpose of a statistic is to define overall excellence or excellence in some aspect of performance. To others, there is a practical concern. How can this statistic be used? Managers, general managers, agents, rotisserie players, gamblers, and everyday players may all view a statistic as valid if it helps them achieve whatever they deem important to the success of their job. To those who take a cerebral approach to baseball, a statistic may be valid if it tells them something about the intricacies of the game that they did not know before or identifies some abstract ability among those who play it. In short, purpose can be almost anything you want it to be.

Generally, however, validity boils down to one thing—*prediction*. Ordinarily, the word *prediction* implies knowledge of the future. In a statistical sense, however, prediction has a much broader meaning: a relationship between two things. Sometimes these are cause-effect relationships. "If the batter singles, a runner on third will score." This is a truth that is timeless. It has been so and shall be so forever. There are other relationships that imply the coexistence of two qualities. "Players who can run fast steal lots of bases." That too is a prediction. If we know one thing is true about a player, we know that the other thing is true without looking it up. In short, prediction means that some relationship exists, knowing that if one condition occurs, the other will occur.

Both of the above examples are valid to the extent that they "predict" that one thing exists or will happen if the other is true. That is the key to validity. Any valid statistic must predict something; otherwise it is just another number. Reliable measures are a dime a dozen. The number of bases on balls plus the number of double plays hit into, divided by the number of strikeouts times the number of sacrifice flies, is as reliable as most other baseball statistics but is not going to attract much attention because it is essentially unrelated to anything that matters.

A correlation between two things also indicates the existence of a relationship. Prediction, then, essentially means correlation. The correlation coefficient is the primary measure by which the validity of a statistic is established. When the broad goal of the statistic is to determine differences between players, a statistic predicts something useful when a list of the players based on the statistic resembles a list of the players on something else. That something else can be almost anything: another statistic, the same statistic from a separate set of circumstances (e.g., future performance during that season or next year), some team event such as wins, something totally outside the actual game (salary, All-Star votes), or whatever. The emphasis, however, is on the criterion and its prediction.

Content Validity

Some forms of validity are not based directly on prediction. Some statistics have de facto validity. Like the cartoon character Popeye, they "am what they am." Batting average is a de facto measure of the tendency to avoid making outs because that is exactly what goes into its definition. Many baseball statistics have at least this kind of validity and used only as de facto measures, do not need further validation. The purpose of the statistic may be simply to indicate which players excel at some aspect of performance. Among the more complex statistics we have discussed so far, speed-power ratio has such a function; it rewards players who hit home runs and steal bases.

Many of these statistics also have *face validity*. The computation of the statistic more or less derives from a logical argument for what qualities that statistic should measure. Thus, statistics supposed to measure "power" contain a heavy dose of home runs and/or other extra-base hits because we believe that those components result from a player's "power." In this case, the criterion is based on various intuitions shared by most baseball people.

Often there is also predictive validity, but the prediction is somewhat trivial. A high slugging average is correlated with (predicts) a large number of home runs. If that were not true, something would be wrong somewhere since home runs (weighted by the factor 4) are the largest determiner of total bases and according to conventional wisdom are what power is all about.

Often face validity is "verified" by comparing the ranked list of players on that statistic with "common knowledge." For example, a list of power hitters that does not include Babe Ruth among the top five would be suspect. However, it is scarcely fair to argue for the validity of a statistic by showing that it meets our intuitions about the ranking of some players, then argue that it is interesting because it produces surprises about the ranking of others. Nevertheless, face validity is also predictive validity in a rather informal way because it correctly "predicts" our intuitions.

Criterion Validity

Technically, however, validity usually means that the statistic correlates with other statistics that are supposed to measure the same thing. Again, correlations of this kind may be relatively trivial. If the two statistics are composed of the same quantities, the correlation may indicate nothing more than the fact that this is the case. The more important correlations are between a statistic and some criterion that does not consist simply of another combination of the same categories from the batting, pitching, and fielding lines.

The trick in any validation procedure is to find such a suitable criterion. Once that is decided upon, the statistical determination of validity is straightforward: Compute the correlation coefficient between the statistic and whatever criterion is being used to validate it. Finding a criterion is not a statistical problem. Criteria, like many things in the world, are in the eye of the beholder. Disagreements about the validity of statistics often reduce to disagreements about which criterion is appropriate. The statistical arguments are factual: which criterion correlates most highly with the measure. That does not make it the *best* criterion, however. Since the choice of a criterion usually depends upon logic, statistical arguments about the statistic may be irrelevant.

There is no inherent reason why statistical measures could not be formally correlated with subjective opinion by using formal rating scales. Such correlations have been staple fare in the behavioral sciences for decades, and in many cases ratings may be appropriate validating criteria in baseball. Fielding ratings, scouting reports, performance awards, Hall of Fame votes, and so on, are already used to some extent. Obtaining reliable ratings involves more than just asking people to rate players from 1 to 10. The technical aspects of developing formal rating procedures will not be discussed here, however, since there are entire books devoted to the subject.

Correlation and Prediction: The Regression Equation

In addition to providing a measure of the relationship between one set of numbers and another, the correlation coefficient may be used to actually predict one value from another. In the case of validity, it means that knowing the value of some statistic, one can estimate the value of the criterion measure. The accuracy of this estimate depends upon how high the correlation coefficient is. If the correlation is 1.00, given a value of the statistic, the corresponding value of the criterion would be known exactly. As the correlation decreases, the prediction is not as accurate, but as long as there is some correlation, the prediction based on the correlation coefficient will be better than a guess.

The correlation coefficient is in terms of a *linear* relationship between the two sets of values. The general equation for a linear relationship:

$$Y = aX + b$$

There are two components to a linear relationship. One component is the *slope (a)*. The slope determines the relationship between the changes in one value and the changes in the other. A linear slope means that the difference between two values in one set is proportional to the difference between the corresponding values in the other. The value of *a* gives that proportion. The second value *(b)* is called the *intercept*. It simply adds a constant to the predicted value. Therefore, it results in a constant difference between two values.

The correlation coefficient is mathematically related to both values. This relationship is in the form of an equation called a *regression equation:*

$$P = a \times O - b$$

where P = the predicted value, O is the value being used to make the prediction. The critical value is *a* (the slope), which is the correlation coefficient *(r)* multiplied by the ratio of the standard deviation of the P's to the standard deviation of the O's.

$$a = r \times (SD_p / SD_o)$$

The additive constant, *b*, is equal to the mean of the predicted values minus the product of the mean of the observed values and *a*.

$$b = M_p - a \times M_o$$

Here is a short set of data from 1990. We will compute the regression equation to predict team runs scored from the team batting average.

Team	BAvg.	Runs
Boston	.272	699
Toronto	.265	767
Seattle	.259	640
Chicago	.258	682
New York	.241	603

Mean BA = .259   Mean Runs = 678.2
SD = .0103   SD = 55.58
$r = .75$
$a = .75 \times (55.58 / .0103) = 4047.09$
$b = 678.2 - (4047.09 \times .259) = -370$

The predicted number of runs for Boston would then be

$$P = (4047 \times .272) - 370 = 1100.81 - 370 = 730.81$$

There is a simple way of measuring how closely the values predicted from a regression equation conform to the actual values. It is called the *standard error of prediction*. It works somewhat like the standard deviation and the standard error. The difference between each predicted value and the actual value obtained by each team is computed, then squared, averaged, and the square root calculated. It is essentially the variability of the obtained values from the predicted values rather than from the mean.

The standard error of prediction is more simply computed, however, by subtracting the square of the correlation coefficient from 1.000 and multiplying by the standard deviation of the values that are being predicted (in the example, the standard deviation of the actual runs scored, or 55.58, *not* the standard deviation of the predicted values).

$$SE_p = SD_p (1 - r^2)$$

Thus, once the correlation coefficient between two statistics is known, the value of either statistic can be predicted from the other and the accuracy of that prediction easily assessed. For our example, the standard deviation was 55.58 and $r = .75$. Therefore, the standard error is

$$SE_p = 55.58 \times (1 - .75^2) = 55.58 \times (1 - .56) = 24.45$$

The units of the standard error are those of the predicted value (runs).

When the correlation is high, the standard error will be small since the square root gets smaller as the correlation coefficient gets larger, with a perfect correlation $SE = 0$. When the correlation is zero, the standard error is equal to the standard deviation of the actual values being predicted.

Interpreting the specific value of a standard error is a tricky business. It is best to find a confidence interval for the accuracy of prediction, just as one computes a confidence interval for some particular statistic. One can be certain of one thing, however. If there is a linear relationship between the two sets of values, predictions from the regression equation are the best that can be made; that is, they produce the smallest value of the standard error that is possible for a linear relation.

The standard error, moreover, provides one criterion for selecting the "best" measure for predicting a particular criterion. The "best" statistic would be the one with the smallest standard error because the size of the standard error reflects the relative accuracy of the predictions.

Validity is not an all-or-none proposition. Validity is defined as the *extent* to which a statistic measures what it should. Thus validity varies in degree, as indicated by the size of the correlation coefficient. If team batting average correlates .87 with team runs scored, it would be considered a "less valid" indicator of total offense than batting runs if the latter correlated .95 with runs scored. Of course, if one wants to know the total offense of a team, it is scarcely necessary to go to the trouble of computing one of the total-offense indexes and using it to predict runs scored. Just look at the runs scored. The value of the statistic comes from the fact that it shows a *relationship* between the combined individual events in the team batting line and runs resulting from those events.

Less than perfect correlations have another interpretation. They indicate the extent to which differences between one set of values are due to differences in the other. Generally, this is known as *common variance* or *shared variance* and is reported as a percentage. The proportion "explained" is equal to the square of the correlation coefficient. If batting average correlates .87 with runs scored, it means that $.87^2$ or 76 percent of the team differences in runs scored may be accounted for by differences in batting average. The remaining 24 percent must be due to something else. If batting runs correlates with runs scored .95, it accounts for 90 percent of the difference.

This is equivalent to saying that there is very little that could be added to the batting runs statistic that would improve its ability to predict runs. If speed-power ratio correlated .27 with runs scored, it accounts for less than 10 percent. These percentages do not mean that the explanation is "apportioned" among the different factors. Speed-power ratio does not account for the remaining 10 percent, just 10 percent in total. Each accounting is an independent estimate for that particular measure. Each measure may also "share variance" with other measures, depending upon their intercorrelation. More about this situation later.

10

Problems in Validation

Validation is not always a simple matter. The very nature of the game and the way its records are kept often defy a straightforward assessment of some kinds of validity. In this chapter we examine some of these problems: determining the validity of offensive and defensive statistics for particular players.

Wins and Runs

The ultimate purpose of baseball is winning games. Therefore, it has been reasonably argued that the test (criterion) of any statistic for individual players is the extent to which it measures a player's contribution to winning games. Individual achievements, such as bushels of strikeouts, may be interesting or even relevant to other criteria (e.g., drawing crowds), but if strikeouts are unrelated to victory, they are strictly for show or show business. The validity of a statistic for the latter purpose might be determined by correlating that statistic to crowd size, but to validate a player's success in playing the game, his performance must be somehow correlated to wins.

Wins, however, are a team statistic and result from two separate aspects of the game, offense and defense. The object of the offense is to score runs, and the object of the defense is to prevent them. For any given game, the team that is more successful at both will outscore the other team and be credited with a win. For any given season, the more often a team scores more runs than the opposition, the greater is its success.

The proportion of games a team wins will be related to the overall difference between the number of runs it scores and the number of runs it allows. Every time a team wins, it outscored its opposition, thus adding to the difference, and every time it loses, it was outscored, thus subtracting from the difference. In fact, if the margins of victory and the margins of defeat are on the average the same, the number of wins will be exactly proportional to the final difference in runs scored and allowed. In other words, the relationship between wins and the difference in runs scored and allowed would be linear and perfectly correlated.

Various equations have been proposed to describe the relationship between runs and wins mathematically. Two will be discussed at this point. The first equation, proposed by Arnold Soolman, is a linear equation:

Winning percentage = (.102 × runs − .103 × runs allowed) / games played + .505

Basically, this equation says that you start with a value of .505 (presumably because teams that score and allow an equal number of runs win slightly more often than they lose) and add a proportional amount for each run scored and subtract a proportional amount for each run allowed.

The second equation, devised by Bill James, is popularly known as the Pythagorean theorem and is the one used by most baseball analysts.

Winning percentage = Runs² / (Runs² + Runs Allowed²)

James's equation is not linear. (Technically, it is known as *hyperbolic;* see Chapter 11.) As long as a league is competitive, as most modern professional leagues are, the linear relation will hold for all teams. If a league is badly out of balance (e.g., one or two teams are totally outclassed), some teams will lose games by a large margin and win by a small margin. In other words, several "surplus" runs will be scored in a lot of games. After a certain point, a large number of runs scored or allowed will not change the outcome of games. The Pythagorean equation takes this nonlinearity into account, hence gives a better prediction in extreme cases, whereas the linear equation may even predict more wins or losses than games played if the difference in runs scored and allowed is large enough.

The validation procedure for each equation would consist of computing the predicted wins according to the equation for a substantial number of teams and comparing these predictions with the actual wins obtained by each team. The standard error of prediction, in this case computed directly from the differences between predicted and obtained values, would provide a good measure of the relative accuracy.

The use of a large number and broad range of observations in any attempt to validate a statistic is extremely important. Numbers computed for a small series of games are highly variable because these runs and wins both contain unsystematic variance. It is not difficult to find unusual cases involving a few games that seem to belie the validity of win predictions. For example, it is not unknown for the losing team in the World Series to outscore the winning team over the entire series. One blowout amid several close games will do it.

In 1946, Hollywood and Los Angeles in the Pacific Coast League played a seven-game series in which each team scored 30 runs. Yet Los Angeles won six of the seven games. Over a large number of games under a wide variety of conditions, the effect of a few anomalies become diluted, but in a small number of games one extremely discrepant case can have a huge effect. The Pythagorean theorem will fare better in these cases.

In validating team statistics on wins and losses, it is sound statistical practice not to include teams from the same league season in a validating sample. The reason is that wins and losses and runs scored and allowed are *not independent* from team to team. In other words, every run scored for one team is a run allowed by another, and every game won by one team is a game lost by another. This means that each team's totals do not represent an independent assessment of the relationship. Perhaps this effect could best be seen in a World Series, where there are only two teams. The data for one team is necessarily a mirror image of that for the other, so you really only have one "example," not two.

The purpose of using a large sample of teams to assess validity is to provide a wide variety of independent cases. Therefore, the sample should be selected to include teams with as broad a range of won-lost records as possible.

Validating Batting Statistics

Since runs scored is related to wins, it is assumed to provide a criterion for validating offensive statistics at the team level. The assumption that a team's runs scored are a weighted combination of individual offensive events has been the primary motivating force behind the development of most offensive statistics such as total offense, total average, batting runs, and runs created. The only problem has been to find the "perfect" combination of categories and weights. That combination will be the one that has good reliability, correlates 1.00 with team runs scored, and is not a computational monstrosity. Offensive (batter) statistics of any kind may be legitimately validated by correlating the statistic for the team with team runs scored.

Again, however, any serious attempt at validation requires a large number of sample teams with a large range of values of both runs scored and the statistical predictor. In this case, however, it is probably not necessary to restrict selection of teams to one team from a league season. The offensive success of one team does not depend upon that of another, so even teams from the same league season are essentially independent cases.*

*When validation involves teams from different years, one may wish to use values that are relative to the league average for that year. If relative values are desired, the appropriate procedure would be first to convert each of the values being used in the analysis (both the statistic and runs scored) to relative values, then compute the correlation coefficient using the corrected values. The merits of using relative values will be considered later.

In attempting to find a suitable criterion to evaluate offensive statistics for a particular batter, one runs into an immediate problem in selecting a suitable criterion. A run scored or batted in cannot be credited to merely one batter (except for a home run) but is the consequence of a sequence of actions by several batters, some of whom may not be credited at all for their contribution. The classic example is a batter who singles a runner from first to third, allowing him to score on a sacrifice fly. He receives credit for neither a run scored nor a run batted in.

This renders the runs scored, runs batted in, or their combination logically poor (nonvalid?) measures of a player's actual contribution to team scoring since they record only the termination of what is often a long sequence of events. This creates a statistical enigma. To evaluate a particular statistic as a measure of offensive proficiency, it is necessary to know how well it correlates with runs, yet runs scored or runs batted in lack logical validity for evaluating individual batters.

In a strict sense, there is no suitable predictive performance criterion for a statistic for individual players. The validity of those statistics must be assumed by the ability of the statistic to predict successfully at the team level. For statistics that are additive at the team level, the team statistic is a sum of the individual contributions weighted by each individual's at-bats or plate appearances. Therefore, the *predicted* runs for a team are a weighted sum of the predicted runs for each individual player, just as the actual runs for a team are a sum of the actual runs scored by each player.

If one applies the regression equation based on the team statistic to each individual on the roster and weights each player's predicted runs by the proportion of at-bats or plate appearances that he contributes to the total, the sum of predicted runs scored will equal the team's total predicted runs (i.e., the number of runs predicted by the regression equation based on team totals). This will be true regardless of the correlation. In this sense, the individual statistic "predicts" as well as the team statistic of which it is a part.

With batting runs, the situation is even simpler. The sum of batting runs for each player is equal to the batting runs computed for the team. Weighting is not necessary because the values for the individual player are not weighted by plate appearances.* Again, these sums are *predicted* runs, not actual runs scored. The predicted runs are apportioned among players in the same way regardless of the accuracy of the regression equation.

This relationship between team and individual achievement does not hold for all statistics. Whenever individual values are not proportional to

---

*If you wanted to add up the individual batting runs to get predicted team batting runs, you would have to correct the player values for the fact that they are in terms of deviations from the league average. It is a fairly simple procedure. Find the league average runs per plate appearance and the player's average batting runs per plate appearance. Add the two values, then multiply by the player's plate appearances to get the predicted runs contributed by that player.

team values, the predicted values for individual players are not proportional either. Additivity at the team level is a necessary prerequisite for this to occur. Thus, there is some question about whether the validity of statistics such as runs created at the team level is relevant to their validity for individual players.

One bit of fallout from this procedure is that any additive offensive statistic for a player may be "converted" to runs by applying the regression equation and multiplying the proportion of total at-bats or plate appearances the player contributes to the team total. For example, Wade Boggs had a batting average of .302 in 619 at-bats. Using the regression equation for team runs scored and batting average developed earlier, Boggs's predicted runs would be

$$Runs = 4047.09 \times .302 - 370 = 852.2$$

In a sense, this is saying that if Boston had a team composed of Wade Boggs clones, they would be predicted to score 852 runs in 5516 at-bats. The average predicted runs per at-bat was therefore 852 / 5516 = .155. Boggs, however, actually had only 619 at-bats. Therefore, his actual contribution was 619 × .155 = 96.0 of Boston's predicted total of 730.8 runs.*

Evaluating Defense

Defense is a confounded combination of pitching and fielding, thus creating content and logical validity problems for any measure. A slow-footed outfield and immobile infield or a spectacular shortstop with miles of range has as much to do with a pitcher's performance as the quality of his pitching. Likewise, the frequency and difficulty of a player's fielding chances depend considerably on the ability and proficiency of the pitcher. A pitcher can kill the best fielder's statistics by allowing batters to drive the ball consistently, while a skilled sinkerball hurler produces two-hoppers to the shortstop.

The batter is much more on his own, and except for runs scored and runs batted in, the various quantities in the batting line are much less affected by the performance of his colleagues than those of the pitcher and fielders. There is no logical reason why pitching and fielding should not be separable, but the items in the pitching line and fielding line do not permit

---

*Some analysts convert potential runs to "batting wins." Since it takes about 10 runs to produce one extra win, runs produced divided by 10 yields wins. This step seems gratuitous. It is basically a simple change in units. It accomplishes little, and intuitively potential runs created by a batter has more meaning than wins.

this separation. With this interpretive limitation in mind, one can still attempt to determine the predictive validity of both pitching and fielding statistics.

Pitching

The purpose of the pitcher, and indeed all other players on defense, is to prevent runs. The team earned run average, which is a proportional composite of each pitcher's individual earned runs and innings pitched, is a direct measure of pitching effectiveness for that team, and it would be redundant to correlate the team earned run average to team earned runs allowed.

This may be a case, however, where it is not completely appropriate to assume that the near perfect correlation at the team level justifies validity at the individual level. Inequities in the assignment of earned runs and the other problems associated with the earned run average discussed in previous chapters erode the logical validity of individual earned run averages as a measure of pitching performance.

In theory, however, one could assess the validity of pitching runs determined from linear weights or any of the mirrored batting statistics for pitchers by using the same procedure that was used for assessing the validity of batting measures—by computing the correlation between team values and team runs allowed.

Fielding

Validation of fielding data is not possible, at least from the fielding line. There is no objective criterion by which any measure of fielding can be compared other than our intuitions about the identity of the best fielders, and there is some weight to the argument that a formalized rating system (e.g., Golden Glove awards) is the best way to handle this problem. Calculations for fielding runs based on fielding chances have no counterpart at the team level.

A fielding chance is not like a hit or a walk. A batter gets credited with a plate appearance every time he goes up to hit no matter what he does, and a pitcher gets credit for a batter faced regardless of what happens to that batter. But a fielder does not have the opportunity to receive a fielding chance on every plate appearance. That will depend on whether the ball is hit in his direction, and that is not up to him. He may have some effect on chances by showing more range, but that is only part of what determines his fielding chances. Moreover, there are only 27 outs (give or take a few) possible in a game. A sluggish middle infield will produce more chances for the other fielders because *someone* has to record those outs. Concentrating on total chances, whether "corrected" by games or even time played, undoubtedly provides a different measure of fielding performance than concentrating on errors (fielding average) but still does not provide an unbiased metric for measuring fielding prowess.

Fielding defense is a team proposition, full of intangibles such as hitting cutoff men and so on, which may be as important as making outs for preventing runs. The problem is a complex one that requires more than the fielding line for its resolution.

Any statistic may be "validated" against team runs allowed according to the procedures already described, providing they are in some way proportional to the team value of the statistic. More complexity is involved in the case of fielding, however, because different positions must logically be treated differently.

Nonstatistical problems abound in determining how positions are to be treated and various quantities weighted. For example, first basemen record as much as 25 percent of the total putouts, but all that is involved is catching a thrown ball. in some computations, assists are weighted more heavily for infielders because it is assumed to be harder to record an assist than a putout. Without some external criterion to evaluate such efforts, there is little to choose between one weighting and another.

Fielding continues to be an enigma because the official data from the fielding line do not seem to provide much valid information. The lack of logical validity in these data has been widely accepted for a long time. Any successful attempt to deal with fielding will require a change in the data, which requires a change in the scoring rules. The first step would be to define a *fielding chance* independent of what the fielder does—for example, any ball hit within a certain distance of a fielder with a certain velocity. Until systematic data of these kinds are generally available, fielding will continue to be the neglected cousin in baseball statistics.*

Reliability and Validity

Although the concept of validity seems simple enough, discussions occasionally can become murky because it is not always clear when validity has been achieved. Part of the cause is the fact that choices of criteria are often a confounded combination of theory, logical assumption, and statis-

*Data of these kinds have recently begun to be published by commercial statisticians. They will be discussed in a later chapter.

tical computation. An almost impenetrable problem arises from the relationship between reliability and validity.

Reliability and validity are closely wedded in evaluating any statistic. If a measure is fallible and contains a large proportion of unsystematic error, it will not be of much use in predicting anything. Predictions of team scoring and team run prevention based on team statistics involve a substantial number of plate appearances or batters faced, usually about 6000 per season. On that basis alone, the reliability of various statistics for a team may be quite high compared with that for a single player, who at most may have about a tenth of that number of plate appearances. The fact that high correlations are obtained with team statistics does not guarantee that level of validity for individual players. Moreover, runs scored is itself subject to some variation due to unsystematic error. The probability of a run scoring on any given plate appearance is .114. For 6000 plate appearances, the standard error for runs would be about .004, or about 25 runs per team in a season. A 95 percent confidence interval for runs would therefore be on the order of 50 runs either way.

Since there is no actual criterion measure for individual players, the accuracy of actual prediction for players cannot be ascertained. The fact that they sum to the team total of predicted runs is not a guarantee of individual accuracy. The additive nature of the statistic makes that happen, not something inherent in the structure of baseball. In a full season, a player has about 500 to 600 plate appearances. If one argued that the ability of the team statistic to predict team runs validates the ability of the individual statistic to predict individual runs (were they to exist), it would be more appropriate to compute the correlation coefficient for samples of team plate appearances of the same size as those of individual players. These validity coefficients based on 600 instead of 6000 plate appearances would more closely resemble the ones that would be obtained if there were a suitable criterion measure for individual players.

To complicate the situation even more, there are different philosophies about validation. A correction formula called the *correction for attenuation* tells you what the validity would be if there was no unsystematic error in *either* measure.

$$Vt = Vo / SQRT (Rc \times Rs)$$

where Vt is the true validity, Vo is the computed correlation between the statistic and criterion, and Rc and Rs are the respective reliabilities. If the reliabilities are 1.00, the obtained validity coefficient is equal to the true coefficient. The very existence of this relationship states that the obtained validity coefficient cannot exceed the combined reliabilities of the two measures.

This is where philosophy comes in. Some experts in measurement suggest that the important thing about a statistic is not simply its ability to predict one fallible measure (runs scored) from another fallible measure (the statistic) but its ability to predict the true value of the criterion no matter how fallible the predicting statistic might be. Therefore, if you are just interested in prediction, you should not correct for lack of reliability in the statistic but only for that in the criterion. In this case, it would be the reliability of runs scored that is important, and in the correction for attenuation, Rs would be eliminated (treated as if it were 1.00).

Validity is not a simple problem, and a suitable procedure for evaluating the predictive ability of individual statistics has yet to be determined. At the same time, the whole purpose of statistics may be thought of as prediction because a statistic that is not related to *something* is useless. Even if it provides nothing more than a verification of our intuitions, predictive validity of some kind is the essence of statistical analysis.

Even reliability ultimately reduces to prediction—the ability of a statistic to predict itself. There is scarcely a question in baseball that cannot be reduced to this simple concept, but in scarcely a question in baseball is it satisfactorily achieved.

11

More on Prediction

Prediction is nothing more than stating a relationship between two things. A correlation coefficient is a predictive statistic. The regression equation derived from the correlation coefficient states the relationship in exact mathematical form, an equation that "predicts" various values of one factor for each value of another. Regression equations are linear. To express a relationship between two things in terms of the correlation cofficient or a regression equation expresses that relationship as a straight line. For every increase in X, there is a proportional increase in Y.

In Chapter 9, the procedure for deriving a regression equation from the correlation coefficient was described. The procedure provides what is called a *least squares equation*. The linear equation that results is the best possible *linear* equation; the sum of the squared deviations between the predicted values of Y and the actual values of Y is as small as it can be.

Many baseball statistics involve relationships that are linear or approximately linear. Descriptive statistics often consist of the sum or weighted sum of proportions or frequencies and hence are a linear combination of the individual values. Batting runs is even known in some quarters as *linear weights*. Some relationships are not linear, however; changes in one factor are not exactly proportional to changes in the other.

Predictive equations are described in terms of three properties: *slope, acceleration,* and *asymptote.* For any equation that predicts Y from values of X, these properties are as follows:

Slope: When Y increases as X increases, Y is said to have a *positive slope.* When Y decreases as X increases, it is said to have a *negative slope.* The relationship between team runs scored and wins has a positive slope. The relationship between team earned run average and wins has a negative slope.

Acceleration: When the increases or decreases in Y become larger and larger as X increases, the relationship is said to be *positively accelerated.* When the increases or decreases in Y become smaller and smaller as X increases, the relationship is said to be *negatively accelerated.* A *linear* relationship is *uniformly accelerated.* The relationship between runs scored per game and wins is negatively accelerated because the value of scoring runs decreases, the more runs you have already scored.

Asymptote: An asymptote is a value that represents the largest or smallest value of Y that can occur. Statistics that are in the form of proportions (e.g., wins) have an asymptote of 100 percent. Actually, no matter how large X gets, Y can never quite reach the asymptote but only comes very close with large values of X.

In addition to slope and acceleration, prediction equations may or may not contain an *additive constant*. This affects the location of values by adding or subtracting a constant amount to each predicted value, Y.

There are a number of different forms of relationships, and each has its special characteristics. Some typical prediction equations and some of their characteristics are listed below. The additive constant has not been included unless there are special reasons for mentioning it. See the figure on the next page for a graphic description of each equation.

1. $Y = a \times^b$

This equation depends mostly on the exponent b. When b is 1, the equation is linear. When b is positive, the slope is positive, and when it is greater than 1, the relationship is positively accelerated. When b is positive and less than 1, it is negatively accelerated. This is a "root" equation. For example, $Y = aX^{.5}$ states that Y is equal to the square root of X. When b is less than zero, the slope is negative, and the function is negatively accelerated, eventually becoming asymptotic at zero. No matter what value of b is used, when $X = 1$, $Y = a$.

The *park factor* (PF) is essentially the ratio of runs scored and allowed at home to runs scored and allowed on the road. Multiplying a batting average by the square root of PF results in an adjusted batting average for a particular player. The effect of PF on batting average may be seen by computing adjusted batting average, Y, for different values of $PF^{.5}$ for any arbitrary batting average a.

2. $Y = aK^{bX}$

In its most useful form K is taken as e, the base of the natural logarithm, or as 10, the base of "normal" logarithms. When b is positive, the slope and acceleration are positive. When b is negative, the slope and acceleration are negative. When X is zero, $Y = a$. When b is negative, the asymptote is zero.

3. $Y = c - aK^{-bX}$

This is a special case of 2 in which a is used as a negative multiplier and c is a positive additive factor. Without the additive factor, the relationship would have negative slope and negative acceleration. But because it is subtracted from a constant, it has positive slope and negative acceleration with an asymptote of c. If $a = c$, then when $X = 0$, $Y = 0$. Essentially, this is useful when the relationship requires the effect of a value of Y to be proportional to the amount of Y that is left. This is the classic *practice curve*. It is generally true that as a player's

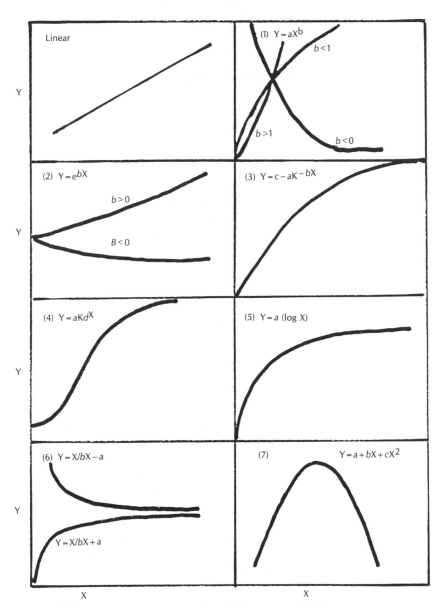

performance improves with practice, the degree of improvement is proportional to the remaining possible improvement.

4. $Y = aK^c$, where $c = d^X$

This is a double exponent where the exponent itself is raised to a power. This relationship is useful because with values of K that are less than .36, it bends twice, being positively accelerated with small values of X, then becomes negatively accelerated for larger values. It has an upper limit equal to a. When $X = 0$, $Y = aK$ (linear).

5. $Y = a \log X$

This is the basic logarithmic relationship. It is essentially a linear equation in which $X = \log X$. The result is that the relationship is negatively accelerated, and when $X = 1$, $Y = 0$.

6. $Y = X / (aX + K)$

This relationship, called *hyperbolic*, is negatively accelerated. It has a positive slope when b is positive and a negative slope when b is negative. The asymptote is $1/a$.

The Pythagorean equation for predicting wins from runs scored and allowed is a special form of 6 in which $X = R^2$, the square of the number of runs scored, and K is a constant equal to the square of the number of runs allowed (RA^2); $a = 1$. A graphic description of the predicted values would show a set of negatively accelerated functions relating wins to runs scored, one for each different value of K (runs allowed). Each function starts at zero when R and hence $R^2 = 0$ and reaches an asymptote of $1/a = 1$ when R is very large with respect to K. (The label *Pythagorean* is something of a curiosity and probably stems from the fact that both variables in the equation are expressed as squares.)

In actual data, the values of R and BA are usually very large, but with data from major league seasons, their range is relatively small. Therefore, only a small segment of the whole equation is actually used. That segment is approximately linear with respect to both X and b, and for all practical purposes a linear function may serve just as well. In truth, however, it is ever so slightly negatively accelerated, and if a league is badly out of balance (e.g., high school, college, or youth leagues) or small and special sets of games are being analyzed, so that there are large differences between runs scored and runs allowed for one or more teams, the lack of linearity contained in the Pythagorean equation may be important.

7. $Y = a + bX + cX^2 + dX^3 + \text{etc.}$

This looks like a linear equation but is actually the most complex of all. If the constants are chosen appropriately, it will predict a slope that changes from positive to negative or vice versa. If it is graphed, it may resemble an arc. Usually this requires a and b to be positive and c to be negative.

Applications

There are two steps in developing an equation to describe a relationship. The first is to choose the form of the equation. Often this involves little more than plotting the relationship on graph paper and trying to match the form it takes to that of some standard equation. A knowledge of the properties of various equations and some properties of the data is of immense help in this process. Sometimes there are logical or theoretical considerations. For example, a linear relation between wins and runs is considered inappropriate by some because it "predicts" that with a large enough difference between runs scored and allowed, the win or loss rate will exceed 100 percent. It is often possible to "match" theoretical restrictions to the properties of the equation. Such things as what happens when $X = 0$, what is the asymptote, what do we know about the acceleration or deceleration of the relationship, and so on may provide a rational starting point.

In some cases, it is possible not only to determine the suitability of a particular equation but even to obtain *least squares* values for the constants. The method consists of transforming the equation into a linear equation, then finding the slope and intercept for the linear form, using the procedures described in Chapter 9 for linear equations. We will not work through the computational procedures, but here is an example of the transformation process.

$Y = aX^b$ may be made linear by taking the logarithm of both sides of the equation so that it becomes $\log Y = \log a + b \log X$. It is now a fairly direct procedure to obtain b and a from the correlation coefficient computed between $\log X$ and $\log Y$. The resulting values will be the best obtainable constants for the *straight line* equation. If the values of $\log X$ and $\log Y$ are plotted on a graph, it is usually obvious whether a straight line is appropriate. If you make this graph and do not get a straight line, then the equation $Y = aX^b$ is not a valid one for those data.

While the constants found by this method produce the smallest possible standard error of prediction for the log equation, they may not produce the best fit for the original data. However, they should be close enough to provide an excellent starting point. Even with a home computer it is possible to check out variations from the least squares values applied to the original equation and note changes to the residual squared deviations from the predicted values. It is then just a tedious trial-and-error process to find values that give the best predictions. Modifications may be made in both constants in various directions until the smallest standard error of prediction is found.*

Multiple Regression

Most predictions in baseball are carried out by correlating a single measure (batting average, slugging average, batting runs) to some criterion

*Detailed computational procedures may be found for all of the equation forms listed above in Lewis' "Quantitative Methods in Psychology."

value (runs scored). While it is true that most statistics are composed of weighted combinations of the frequencies in various categories, the combination has largely been rational, guided by some kind of more or less logical or theoretical assumptions about what is important and what is not.

It is also possible to predict the criterion directly from the weighted sum of individual values, with the weights determined mathematically to provide the best prediction possible. By "best prediction," we mean that no set of weights could improve on the accuracy of the linear prediction. The procedure is called *multiple regression*. The basic equation of multiple regression:

$$C = a + bX1 + cX2 + dX3 \ldots + KXn$$

where C is the criterion measure; X1, X2, X3 are the frequencies in the various categories from which the prediction is to be made; and *b, c, d* are the weights assigned to those categories. Multiple regression procedures will not identify what X1, X2 should be, but given that we have frequencies in several categories for each player (or team) and a criterion measure (runs scored), it is possible to find the best weighting of those frequencies that when added together will produce the most accurate prediction of the criterion. Accuracy is defined in terms of the standard error of prediction.

An equation for predicting runs from the frequencies of individual offensive events would resemble the linear weights equation for batting runs; each component is multiplied by a constant and the values summed. In a multiple regression equation, however, there is no restriction that the factors entering into the equation make any rational sense. Some things for which there seems to be no reason could add to the prediction, and some things that rationally should be included might add very little.

The procedure for obtaining regression weights for even two categories is tedious and for more than two categories requires rather high-level mathematical procedures that are best carried out on a computer. Commercial software available for home computers requires no knowledge of how the computations are done, just a faith that the programmer has done his job correctly. We shall not deal with calculations here but discuss the basic principles of multiple regression and illustrate the kind of results that are obtained.

Suppose we have three measures for a number of teams—runs scored, hits, and walks. The goal is to predict runs scored from hits and walks. We begin with the separate correlations between each of the two "predictors" and runs scored. For example, suppose we find that hits correlates with runs .50 and that walks correlates with runs .40. We could compute two regression equations, one for hits, the other for walks. Assuming for simplicity that the intercepts are zero, we have

$R = hX$ (hits) and $R = wX$ (walks), where
$h = .50 \times (SDr / SDh)$ and
$w = .40 \times (SDr / SDw)$

If we think of the correlation coefficient in terms of percentage of variance explained (r^2), hits accounts for 25 percent of the variance and walks for 16 percent. Suppose the correlation between walks and hits was zero. That means that they share no variance between them. Hits accounts for 25 percent and walks for a different 16 percent. We could therefore simply add the two prediction equations together:

$$R = h \times (\text{hits}) + w \times (\text{walks})$$

Suppose, however, that hits and walks are themselves correlated .50. That means that 25 percent of the variance in each measure is shared. Now if we simply add the two shares together to account for the variance in runs, that 25 percent of the variance in each measure is being counted twice, once in hits and again in walks. The diagram on the following page makes this clear.

The first set of circles indicates that runs shares 25 percent of the variance with hits and 16 percent with walks. Since there is no variance shared between hits and walks, the two components do not overlap, and each accounts for its portion. When the two measures are correlated, they overlap, as in the second set of circles. The section that the three factors share will be counted twice—once in the hits equation and once in the walks equation. Therefore, this overlapping portion has to be subtracted from the total variance to get the amount contributed by hits and walks—that amount of runs "taken up" by the two overlapping circles. The remaining part, not covered by either hits or walks, is called the *residual*. It represents the inaccuracy of the prediction. With only a small variation in runs attributable to hits and walks, we would not be able to predict runs very well from just those two quantities; runs scored would vary considerably from the predicted values because there are a lot of factors that affect runs that are not being taken into account when we use just hits and walks to predict them.

Multiple regression procedures simply "adjust" the constants h and w to eliminate the common variance, still maintaining the basic criterion of keeping the residual, as measured by the difference between predicted and obtained values, as small as possible.

Now suppose we add a third predictor to our equation, say stolen bases. In the terms of the diagram, prediction will be improved by using up more of the residual. Suppose we find that stolen bases correlates with runs scored .32. That means that it will consume 10 percent of the total variance. If it is

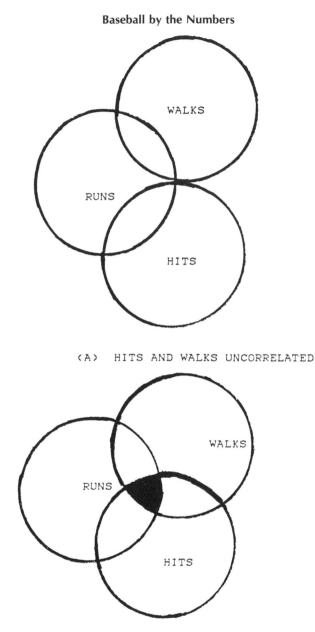

(A)   HITS AND WALKS UNCORRELATED

(B) HITS AND WALKS CORRELATED

uncorrelated with either hits or walks, it will take that 10 percent out of the residual. It cannot overlap with either of the circles representing those factors unless it is correlated with either or both of them. If it is correlated with the original predictors, it must be drawn to account for that overlap. Therefore, if you add a measure that is poorly correlated with the criterion, it will not take up much of the runs circle. If it is highly correlated with other measures, it may take up a lot of space, but that space has already been taken by the other measures, and little predictability is added.

Most analytic computer programs will provide several relevant values. The most important single value is the multiple correlation coefficient. The correlation coefficient is one way to indicate how good the prediction is because its square provides a measure of the variance being accounted for by that particular constellation of predictors and weights. Graphically, it would be the percentage of the circle for runs that is taken up by the overlapping circles representing the predictors.

For actual predictions, however, it is the weights of the various factors entering into the regression equation that provide the practical significance of the analysis. Given the weights, it is a simple matter to take the obtained values of the various predictors, multiply each one by its weight, and add them to get predicted runs scored.

A multiple regression analysis for teams might produce an equation that looks like this:

$$\text{Runs} = (.49 \times 1B) + (.56 \times 2B) + (2.01 \times 3B) + (1.90 \times HR) + (.31 \times BB + HP) + (.05 \times SH) + (.0007) \times SB) - (.17 \times SO) - (.03 \times CS) - (.25 \times DP) - 241.79$$

To get the predicted number of runs scored for a team, you would simply multiply the frequency in each category by the appropriate weight and sum the results. The multiple correlation coefficient for these weights is .952, which accounts for 90 percent of the variance. If the standard error of estimate computed from the difference between the obtained and predicted values was 15, it would mean that about two-thirds of the predicted values would be within 15 runs of the actual values.*

No theoretical considerations are involved in this example. We simply took all of the quantities in the batting line and entered them into the multiple regression equation. The resulting equation is an expression of the best *linear* prediction involving those categories. It is inappropriate to consider these weights as valid indicators for individual players, however. The multiple regression equation is simply a description of a set of results. The weights do not take into account differences in plate appearances. If each quantity had been divided by plate appearances, a different set of weights would have been generated. If predictions for individual players were made, weights based on plate appearances would probably be more appropriate.

To make matters even more complicated, there are two forms of multiple regression. In the standard procedure, the one used in the example,

---

*Soolman's equation for predicting wins from runs scored and allowed is a multiple regression equation, and hence for his data gives the best linear predictions possible. For other sets of data, other constants may prove to be more accurate.

each factor is evaluated in terms of what it adds to the predictability over and above all the other factors—in other words, how much unique space it takes in the circle.

In the other form called *hierarchical analysis,* the factors are added one at a time and are evaluated in terms of what they contribute to what is left *at the time.* The order in which they are entered is extremely important and is determined by theoretical importance. For example, one could start with the assumption that bases gained is the most important determiner of runs scored, enter that value first, then add strikeouts to see if they add any substantive predictability. Conversely, it is possible to consider the first factors entered as "control" factors. For example, one might be able to enter singles first and enter total bases second to examine the importance of total bases with the effect of singles removed.*

Outliers

Outliers are essentially cases that do not fit the rest of the data. The most famous outliers of all time were the Cleveland Spiders of 1899, who won only 20 games and lost 134, for a won-lost proportion of .149. The next worst record in history was 16 games better. In statistical terms, outliers are generally considered cases that are more than 3 standard deviations from the mean. This does not necessarily mean that they are "weird" cases because about in 1 in 1000 cases will be that far out based on random sampling. However, if that one case occurs in a small set of 25 or so cases, it can have a serious effect on predictive equations based on the least squares criterion.

Extreme values always exert a tremendous influence on any averaging procedure. For example, the Spiders gave up 1252 runs, an average of over 8 per game, almost double that of the league leaders and about 30 percent more than the next worst team. Any linear prediction equation that included the Spiders would be seriously affected by this one extreme value. It would still be the best possible linear prediction on the average, but to come anywhere near this one value, the best straight line would not follow the trer··· established by all the other teams. It is somewhat like averaging the salar, of four statisticians with that of the president of General Motors. The sum

---

Hierarchical analysis contains several pitfalls and should not be attempted by the unwary. For example, suppose in trying to predict runs we enter slugging average first as a "control" factor, then enter home runs. If we found that home runs added little predictability, it would not be correct to conclude that home runs are unimportant. In a sense, we have already "used up" the home run variance because it is an integral part of slugging average. Because baseball measures are always composed of the same categories, the problem of unconfounding their parts is one of the most difficult problems facing baseball analysts.

of deviations from the mean would still be zero, but the mean would not be near any value in the set and not typical of the group.

There are two opposing views about what to do about outliers. Some analysts consider it a challenge to find a nonlinear function that will come close to predicting both the outlier and the rest of the data. For example, a function that is almost linear through most of its range but has a sharp inflection at the extremes may provide a decent description of the results, including the outlier. The other view is that these highly unusual cases are atypical and occur so seldom that predicting their occurrence is of little practical or scientific value. Eliminating them from the analysis is considered "cleaning up the data" to develop predictive formulae that will be more accurate for 999 out of 1000 cases. It is a rather democratic policy of sacrificing the few for the good of the many.

There is an old saying about equations: "With enough constants, you can predict an elephant." An equation of the form $Y = a + bX + cX^2 \ldots + dX^n$ will provide almost perfect prediction for n cases. Outliers can be predicted, but it often requires adding an extra constant or making the prediction equation more complex. The purpose of statistics is to reduce complexity, not to take something simple and describe it in complex terms in order to be perfectly accurate. Predicting wins from runs scored and allowed is bound to be accurate if a separate constant is used for each case.

12

Evaluating Systematic Effects

Statistical procedures are most useful in dealing with unsystematic and random influences on performance over a specified series of plate appearances or batters faced. Estimates of unsystematic error are easily obtained and their effects definable. Systematic factors are a much more complicated problem.

We will approach the problem by returning to the basic measurement equation:

$$Var(X) = Var(T) + Var(E)$$

The E component is defined by those factors that will balance out in the long run. The sum of errors over a large number of plate appearances is zero, so that variation due to error will evaporate. In the short run, the contribution of Var(E) to the measured differences between players is measured by the reliability and the standard error.

We have pointed out before that Var(T) results from several factors. They are included in T simply because they will contribute to differences between players without averaging out across plate appearances, no matter how many plate appearances a player may have. These components fall into two broad classes: (1) those contributed by the player himself (abilities, skills, motivation, etc.); (2) those determined by differences in conditions under which players play (the park, day vs. night, liveliness of the ball, height of the mound, umpiring, strategy, weather, etc.). Within a defined set of at-bats, some or all of these factors may be random, but for some comparisons between players they differ systematically from player to player and hence contribute to Var(T).

The basic equation may thus be rewritten as

$$Var(X) = Var(P) + Var(C) + Var(E)$$

Since the playing conditions (C-factors) contribute to "true variance," some researchers consider them an undesirable part of Var(X). The argument is that the goal of evaluating players is to evaluate them in terms of their skills and abilities (the P factors). The C-factors, if they cannot randomize out, vary systematically from player to player and will bias this assessment.

Sometimes this problem has been phrased as "How many homeruns would Willie Mays have hit if he had played home games in Atlanta Stadium?" or "What would Lou Boudreau's batting average have been if he had had to bat against the great Cleveland pitching staff?" or "What would Bob Feller's record have been if he had not spent the war years in the navy?" Those questions may provide interesting bar entertainment but do the issue a real injustice.

The problem is not simply "what if" but of using statistical procedures to gain a better understanding of what contributes to a player's performance. In some cases, it is virtually a requirement if predictions of future performance are to be accurate. For example, minor league parks, weather, and level of competition differ widely. In attempting to predict major league performance from minor league performance, Bill James took these differences into account. Without such an accounting, prediction would be hopeless.*

Normalizing or Standardizing Values

On occasion, it is interesting to construct a list of players ranked on some statistic when the players in the list played in different seasons. For example, one might wish to compile a list of first-year players in the last decade or a ranked list of all of the league batting champions for the last 20 years. If this is done solely on the basis of obtained values, the differences between players are determined not only by unsystematic error, Var(E), in the statistic, but also by any seasonal differences in the true value. Neither can be avoided, but attempts have been made to adjust or correct the obtained values of the statistic to neutralize some systematic sources of variation that may affect the true component.

Foremost among these procedures are the normalizing or standardizing procedures described in Chapter 6. In particular, converting the player's statistic to a standard score corrects that score for differences in the mean and standard deviation (variance) between the seasons. As long as the seasonal variable has an additive or proportional effect on the true value that is the same for all players, the standard-score procedure removes seasonal variation in the mean and variance from the obtained scores.

The procedure does not distinguish between (1) differences in the mean and variance due to playing conditions and (2) changes in the mean and variance due to overall ability level of the players during a particular season.

---

*As described in Stats 1992 Minor League Handbook, *published by Stats, Inc.*

In other words, it does not discriminate P-factors from C-factors. All that the statistical adjustment does is to express the statistic relative to the mean and variance of the reference group. It does not indicate what made that mean and/or variance differ. This fact complicates the interpretation of relative statistics.

An example or two may clarify the problem. In 1949, the batting average of the National League was .262. Elbie Fletcher of Boston also had a batting average of .262. Therefore, his z-score was zero and could be standardized to 100. In 1989, the National League batting average was .246. Rafael Ramirez of Houston also had a batting average of .246, for a standard score of 100. Now the facts are indisputable. Relative to their respective groups, both players performed the same, exactly at the average.

How one interprets this fact, however, depends upon what determined the difference in league average. If that difference was due entirely to differences in playing conditions, then Fletcher merely played under more favorable circumstances, but both were equal as players. On the other hand, if the higher league batting average in 1949 indicated that the overall caliber of batters was better for that season, then Fletcher was indeed a "better" player than Ramirez, despite the fact that each batted at the mean of his group. In other words, what we think of a player should not be determined by how well his colleagues performed.

It also works the other way. In 1944, during World War II, the National League had a batting average of .261, very close to that in 1949. Goody Rosen of Brooklyn also had a batting average of .261 in 1944. Since the league averages were almost the same, does that mean that there was no difference between those league seasons? This seems unlikely; the talent pool has been assumed to be much poorer during the war. In this case, one would be quite reluctant to take common standard scores of 100 at face value. In other words, it is doubtful that Rosen's standard score of 100 is an indication that he and Fletcher are equally good players.

The point is that it is not certain how much external factors contribute to differences in the two reference groups and how much is contributed by genuine differences between players. Statistical analysis presents us with certain facts, but their interpretation depends upon some very arguable assumptions. Normalizing or standardizing to the league average simply expresses a statistic in relation to the league average. It is not incorrect to say that Fletcher, Ramirez, and Rosen had equally good seasons as long as it is clear what that statement means.*

Standard or normalized values also do not correct for effects that are not

---

*For a somewhat absurd example, my son had a little league batting average that was right at the league average. Is he as good as Fletcher, Ramirez, and Rosen? Obviously not, but relative to the group to which he belonged, his season was equally successful.

the same for all players. If differences in playing conditions affect players differently, then a player's relative score will change irrespective of any changes in the overall mean or standard deviation. If umpires lower the strike zone, pitchers will probably make fewer high pitches, and high-ball hitters will be likely to suffer, low-ball hitters likely to prosper. Some players profit by changing leagues, and others are hurt by the same change. Standardizing a statistic does not have any correcting effect in this case. Nor does standardizing a statistic remove unsystematic error.

Park Effects

There are also biases that occur within a season. The one that has generated the most interest is the *park effect*. The park effect is actually two almost inseparable biases. A player plays half of his games in one field but never faces his team's pitching staff, or for pitchers, his team's batters. The bias results in an increase in the differences between players on different teams and a decrease in the differences between players on the same team. There have been serious attempts to correct a player's obtained statistics for this bias.

Pete Palmer approached the problem by developing a park factor for each team season that is then used as a multiplicative constant to correct batting and pitching statistics for each individual on the team. The derivation of the park factor is ingenious but unbelievably complicated and will not be dealt with here. Essentially, it is the ratio of team runs at home to team runs on the road, and for pitchers, team runs allowed at home to team runs allowed on the road. Various corrections and adjustments are made to obtain the final values. The procedure has been published in several sources, and there are even published lists of park factors (e.g., *Total Baseball*, pp. 2262.) for those who are inclined to make use of the correction.

Because the procedure is so complicated, its exact structure is somewhat obscure, but there are some general properties that are worth noting. Batter-friendly parks have a value greater than 1.00, and pitcher-friendly parks have a value less than 1.00—all relative to the league average.

Park factors are multiplicative corrections and are applied to all batters or pitchers for a team. Depending on the measure, it is used somewhat differently. For batters, either the park factor or sometimes its square root is used as a divisor (except for batting runs, which will be considered momentarily). When used as a divisor, it will proportionally reduce the statistic in a hitter-friendly park. *Example:* In 1987, Dale Murphy had a batting average of .295, and Atlanta Stadium had a park factor of 1.08. Murphy's adjusted batting average would be .295 / 1.08 = .273. Murphy's batting average may also be normalized to the league average: $.295 / .261 \times 100 = 113$, which is then adjusted to $113 / 1.08 = 104.6$. Converting back to batting average, we get $1.046 \times .261 = .273$.

For pitchers, the situation is somewhat confusing. When the measure for a pitcher is such that "larger is poorer," division by the park factor is also appropriate. Bryn Smith's earned run average in 1987 was 4.37. Adjusting for the Olympic Stadium park factor of 1.06 results in an adjusted earned run average of $4.37 / 1.06 = 4.12$. When such a statistic is normalized, it is usually expressed in positive terms, so that larger is better. In this case, the statistic should be multiplied by the park factor. Thus, Smith's normalized earned run average was $4.12 / 4.37 \times 100 = 94$. Adjusted for park effects, it would be $94 \times 1.06 = 99.6$. Converting back to earned run average, we have $.996 \times 4.12 = 4.10$.

In addition:

- For a given park factor, the larger the value of the statistic, the greater the correction. This has two effects: (1) players with larger values of the statistic will be affected more than those with smaller values; (2) statistics that normally have larger values and greater variability (e.g., slugging average) will be affected to a greater extent. This is a valuable property since the variability of those statistics is also larger.
- The park component should change only from year to year when park conditions change.* But personnel changes should require a change in the pitcher-batter portion of the correction annually. Tables therefore report annual values.
- The tabled values are based only on runs scored and given up and are the same regardless of the statistic being considered. There is no provision for the fact that correlations between various statistics and runs scored or yielded may differ. It is also likely that *true* park effects vary for different categories. For example, a park friendly to home run hitters may give up fewer doubles or triples, or even singles, and some categories may be determined more by the pitching contribution than the batting contribution (e.g., walks). In practice, separate park factors should be, and often are, computed for different statistics.
- Because the park effect is assumed to be constant for a particular park, the correction does not take into account the interaction between park and player; that is, park effects may affect some players

*Except in Toronto, where "dome-open vs. dome-closed" games appear to most casual observers to affect the game differently. The use of a common averaged value for Toronto adds some variability to the correction. Park effects may also vary from year to year because of weather differences, differences in travel schedule, and so on.

more than others. In this respect it is just like standardized statistics.

- Since for every run scored by one team, one must be given up by another, the combined park effect is zero (i.e., the average park factors across league parks for any season is 1.00). This is how the correction reduces differences between players on different teams. Because it is a relative effect, the numbers for players on some teams must be adjusted upward and for others downward.

- The validity of the formula for determining park factors is based on its success in predicting home-road run differences from team statistics. Since this was the criterion used in its development, it is not surprising that it is successful at the team level. Because the factor is a multiplicative constant, the sum of adjusted values for individual players will no longer sum to the adjusted total for the team.

- There is no provision for unsystematic error in wins or runs (the park factor's two main components). The park factor is essentially an average value and like all averages is subject to an uncertain amount of unsystematic error. Since it is a fallible measure, it adds unsystematic error to a player's statistics.

  The effect of the transformation on reliability is somewhat uncertain, however. It probably depends on the team-by-team composition of the players in the list. Since the effect of the transformation is to reduce the differences between players from different teams, it will enhance differences between players from the same team when the constant is greater than 1 and reduce differences between players from the same team when the constant is less than 1. Just how these complexities affect a particular set of players is likely to vary considerably.

- Batting runs does not behave quite the same as other statistics. It is in the form of a deviation from the league average. Therefore, it is necessary to convert the value into actual runs before applying the correction. This was discussed briefly in Chapter 4. More completely, the correction is carried out as follows: First find the league average runs per plate appearance (R / PA). The expected number of batting runs for that player is equal to the league average times the number of plate appearances for the batter.

  Example: A batter has 25 batting runs in 600 plate appearances. The league scored 8200 runs in 74,000 plate appearances, for an average of $8200 / 74,000 = .111$ runs per plate appearance. This means that the player should have produced $.111 \times 600 = 66.6$ runs if he was average. Since he had 25 runs above average, his actual value was $66.6 + 25 = 91.6$. If the park factor was 1.1, his home park is 10 percent more favorable to hitters than the average park. Therefore, the expected average would be 1.1×66.6, or 73.3 runs. His production of 91.6 is only $91.6 - 73.3 = 18.3$ above average rather than 25.

$$BR(adj) = BR - League\ Runs / League\ PA \times PF - 1 \times Player\ PA$$

- In theory, a formula based on any identifiable factor that biases comparisons between players could be derived in much the same way as those for park factors—by comparing runs scored and allowed under those conditions. Seasonal corrections could also be made by developing a *season factor* using the ratio of runs scored in one season to that in another.
- The park factor is not a correction for games played in a particular park. It is a correction for a *bias* produced by playing half of the games in one place and never facing one's own pitchers or batters. Therefore, it is applied to totals averaged over a season, not to some particular subset of games in one park. Applying the park factor to just home games would be inappropriate.

Combining Adjusted Values

For some purposes, it may be desirable to obtain an adjusted statistic for plate appearances in more than one home park. For example, a player plays part of the season with one team and part of the season with another, or in his career he plays with several teams.

This involves more than just averaging the value of a statistic. When combining subsets of statistics, it usually makes more sense to weight each value by the number of plate appearances. For example, to obtain a combined batting average, one should correct the number of hits for each subset of plate appearances, then combine the adjusted hits and at-bats into a single value.

Suppose a player had 200 at-bats with 55 hits (avg. .275) playing for one team and 150 at-bats with 35 hits (.233) playing for another team. The park factor for the first team was 1.10 and for the second team .95. First correct the two batting averages: $.275 / 1.10 = .250$; $.233 / .95 = .245$. Convert both to hits: $.250 \times 200 = 50$; $.245 \times 150 = 36.8$.* Then combine the two into a total adjusted batting average: $(50 + 36.8) / 350 = .248$. This results in the total average being weighted by the number of at-bats in each location.

In effect, the same procedure should be used to obtain an adjusted total

---

*Although Palmer recommends using the square root of the park factor for batting averages, the park factor was used here to simplify the example.

across several seasons, as in a career average. If the correction was the same for each season, then only the total need be adjusted, but if the correction factor differs from season to season, each season should be adjusted as above, then the totals combined.

A simple seasonal correction could also be based on normalized or standard scores for the statistic being corrected—for example, batting average. The normalized value is easier to work with and will be used in this example. A player played in three seasons and had batting averages of .280, .310, and .275 in 400, 600, and 300 at-bats. The league's overall batting average for the three seasons combined was .260. The three seasons that the player was in the league, the league had batting averages of .255, .261, and .257. The normalized ratios for these three seasons was −.019, .004, and −.012 (e.g., [.255 − .260] / .260 = −.019, etc.).

The correction factor for the first season would therefore be $1 - .019 = .981$; for the second season, 1.004; and for the third season, .988. The correction is then made as in the example above. First correct the three batting averages (.280 / .981 = .285; .310 / 1.004 = .309; and .275 / .988 = .278). Multiply each adjusted average by the number of at-bats (.285 × 400 = 114; .309 × 600 = 185.4; .275 × 300 = 82.5). The total number of adjusted hits is then divided by the total at-bats: 381.9 / 1300 = .294.

There is no reason why these individual values could not be further adjusted by park factors before combining them if the player played for different teams. Methodologically, analyses of this kind may be as fine-grained as necessary to achieve suitable predictive validity in various situations.

Final Considerations

When indulging in these fantasies, it is important to keep in mind that the real motivation is to remove some factors from the "true value," thus allowing an assessment of the player's performance attributable only to whatever is left. It is therefore important to understand just what has and has not been corrected.

Standard and normalized scores are indiscriminate but limited. The effect of any factor that affects the mean and variance of the values for players on the list is neutralized. This is akin to adding a constant value to the players' scores or multiplying them by a constant value. A player's standing in two lists (seasons) will still be determined by factors that do not produce differences in the overall mean and variance between the two seasons.

When the park factor is based on runs scored and allowed, it is then based on the presumed correlation of offensive events to runs scored. The adjustment is probably most apt when the statistic is both additive over players and highly correlated with runs scored.

In the final analysis, it is the success of predictions made with these kinds of adjustments that determines their value.

13

Situational Effects: Chi-square

With the advent of computer data storage, it has become easier to devise samples of at-bats, plate appearances, or batters faced that differ in some specified characteristic. For example, one can compare home and road games, games against various opponents, various bases-outs situations, even pitching counts. The name *situational statistics* applied to compendia of these results has become almost a buzzword among baseball statisticians. The list of situational statistics is limited only by the ambition and ingenuity of the programmer and the desire of the media, fans, and gamblers for more trivia. Sometimes the questions are focused on evaluating specific players (e.g., who are the best RBI men with runners in scoring position?), and sometimes the focus is on the situation itself (e.g., does artificial turf produce greater base-stealing success?), but in either case, the answer usually requires more than just computing the situational statistic.

Actually, the plate appearances that define situational statistics do not differ in principle from any other subset. When taken in the context of an entire career, a player's seasonal statistics are situational; they represent some segment of his total numbers defined by a season. Procedures for comparing a player's season-by-season record are no different from those used to compare selected sets of plate appearances within a season or a selected set of plate appearances from one season with that from another.

Sometimes these statistics are merely descriptive. In 1989, Eric Davis had a batting average of .318 with runners in scoring position. Like most statistics, that is a fact in itself, but more often such figures are assumed to have some meaning beyond their particularity. When that average is reported along with his .281 career average, the implication is that Davis is generally better in the clutch than otherwise and therefore might be expected to perform the same way in the future. Two kinds of questions exemplify the distinction between particular fact and general statement. "Who had the best and worst second-half on-base averages in 1990?" This is a perfectly legitimate question, easily answered by simply compiling a list of players ranked on on-base average. The list answers the question with no further statistical machinations necessary. Compare this with "Who are the best leadoff hitters in baseball?" This question does not refer to how a player performed in some particular set of games but to what he is like. It assumes that there are good leadoff men and not so good leadoff men and that the data will tell us which is which. A good leadoff man now should be a good leadoff man forever.

To answer this question, the same kind of data is presented—a list of players ranked according to their on-base averages (the assumed criterion for being a good leadoff man) when they are in the leadoff position. Because the focus is on the player (true value) and not just his particular performance, the reliability of the measure becomes critical. It tells us little about the player's leadoff ability if the list contains so much unsystematic (error) variance that differences among players in true scores are obscured. In a sense, the issue again boils down to prediction. Does the list allow us to predict something about the player's performance?

Reliability and evaluation of these lists may be carried out using the methods described in Chapter 7. Procedures apply in the same way to situational, season, or career lists. In general, the number of plate appearances for situational statistics is much smaller than for a full season. Therefore, lower reliabilities and larger standard errors are likely to be the norm for situational lists.

There may be confusion about validity as well. Seasonal lists are defined by criteria that have nothing to do with the games. A season is a season, and there can be little argument about which plate appearances are part of that season and which are part of another. Because situational statistics are often defined by something that happens in a game, the appropriate measure and the criteria defining the particular plate appearances or at-bats included in some situational set may be arguable.

In the above example, one may wish to argue whether on-base average is the best criterion by which to evaluate a leadoff batter. There has already been a great deal of discussion among baseball analysts about the existence of clutch hitters. Many of these arguments are concerned with which plate appearances should be used to define clutch situations. Such arguments often generate more heat than light, but because the choice of criterion is a logical rather than a statistical problem, it should not be confused with the statistical problems involved in verifying the existence of this possibly mythical animal.

Examining some situational factor usually involves a comparison, implied or actual, of one list with another. It is often implied. A list of players ranked on their performance in the second half of the season is interesting only in relation to their performance in the first half. A list of players ranked according to their performance in clutch situations is interesting only with respect to a list of these players in nonclutch situations. Therefore, it is not just the reliability of a single list of players but the comparison of one list with another that is important.

The second aspect of situational statistics of interest is the assessment of the situational factor itself. Is there a general advantage to being in the home park? Is it more advantageous to hit ground balls when playing on a field with natural turf? These questions involve speculation about effects that are not just specific to a few players but presumed to have an effect on all players, and it requires more than just a reliable list of players to determine its effect. It likewise implies a comparison between lists, but in this case the interest may be in the mean performance of all of the players in the list rather than the relative position of the players.

In this and succeeding chapters, we shall be concerned with individual differences in situational effects and the general effect of situational factors. Most questions fall into just a few categories in which standard procedures may be used. Usually, it is the form of the data and the kind of factor that is involved that determine which statistical procedure is applied.

Evaluating Proportions: Introduction to Chi-square

Chi-square is a simple statistic that may often be used to evaluate a single value in proportional form or to compare two or more proportions. By now, you should be used to thinking in terms of the contribution of random error to differences between statistical values. Chi-square is simply another way to determine whether it is likely that a difference is produced by random error. In its simplest form, chi-square is used to evaluate the difference between an obtained proportion and some theoretical proportion.

In his last season with the Phillies, Richie Ashburn had a batting average of .266 (150 hits, 564 at-bats). His career average was .308, which we will assume represents his true average. Is the obtained average of .266 significantly different from .308, or is it likely to be a random variation from that value? Chi-square will provide evidence on this matter. Actually, it operates with the frequencies of the events rather than directly with the proportions. If Ashburn had equaled his career average of .308, he should have had 173.7 hits (.308 $\times$ 564), the expected number of hits in 564 at-bats. In addition, he made 564 − 150 = 414 outs. The expected number of outs is 564 − 173.7 = 390.3. It is not necessary that the expected values be whole numbers since they are theoretical values. Moreover, it is more accurate to carry several decimal places and then round off the final value to two places. The first step in computing chi-square is to subtract the expected values from the obtained values. These are then squared and divided by the expected values.

$$\text{Hits} = (150 - 173.7)^2 / 173.7 = -23.7^2 / 173.7 = 3.23$$
$$\text{Outs} = (414 - 390.3)^2 / 390.3 = 23.7^2 / 390.3 = 1.44$$

Chi-square is the sum of these two values, or 4.67.*

The most important property of chi-square is that we know how large it is likely to be if the difference in proportions is simply a result of random variation. For this example, we would expect values of chi-square to be larger than 3.84 less than 5 percent of the time by chance. Since the obtained chi-square exceeds this value, Ashburn's performance was significantly deviant from his long-term average.

Where did we obtain the value 3.84? Critical values of chi-square for various situations have been compiled in tables. Table 2 in Appendix C provides several important criteria—the values of chi-square that will be exceeded 20 percent, 10 percent, 5 percent, and 1 percent by random variation. These are listed in the columns. The rows refer to a mysterious quantity called *degrees of freedom*. At this point it is not important to know what degrees of freedom really are or why they are there. Their presence indicates that the criteria values of chi-square depend upon how many comparisons are being made. Degrees of freedom (d.f.) are 1 less than the number of comparisons. Since we are comparing hits and outs, there is 1 d.f., and the critical value of chi-square of 3.84 for 5 percent is found in the third column of the first row.

Even though the chi-square computed on the proportion of Ashburn's hits and outs exceeded the tabled value, chance alone will produce a chi-square this large almost 5 percent of the time.

Comparing Two Conditions for a Single Player

In 1989, Wade Boggs had 113 hits in 300 at-bats in Fenway Park (.377) and 92 hits in 321 at-bats on the road (.287). Was Boggs really that much of a "homer," or is this likely to be an effect of random variation? Chi-square may be used to provide some evidence on this question.

Boggs's overall batting average was 205 / 621 = .330. Therefore, if he had the same batting average at home and on the road, he would have obtained .330 × 300 = 99 hits at home and .330 × 321 = 105.93 hits on the road.

In evaluating a single player, the assumption is made that successive plate appearances are independent. In other words, it is as if the batter simply rolled the dice every time he came to the plate and the odds did not change. While there are several reasons for believing that this assumption is not true, the data appear to behave as if each plate appearance was unaffected by the results of previous plate appearances. Nevertheless, considerable caution is advised in applying chi-square to a set of plate appearances all obtained from a single batter. In Chapter 18 we shall examine some procedures that may be used to determine whether successive plate appearances are independent.

These are the *expected* numbers of hits. Boggs made $300 - 113 = 187$ outs at home and $321 - 92 = 229$ outs on the road. The expected number of outs would be $300 - 99 = 201$ outs at home and $321 - 105.93 = 215.07$ outs on the road. Chi-square is then computed exactly as in the first example.

Hits (home) $= (113 - 99)^2 / 99 = 14^2 / 99 = 1.98$
Outs (home) $= (187 - 201)^2 / 201 = -14^2 / 201 = .98$
Hits (road) $= (92 - 105.93)^2 / 105.93 = -13.93^2 / 105.93 = 1.83$
Outs (road) $= (229 - 215.07)^2 / 215.07 = 13.93^2 / 215.07 = .90$

Chi-square is again the sum of these four values, or 5.69. In this case, the degrees of freedom are the product of the number of conditions minus 1 and the number of comparisons minus 1. Since there are two conditions (home vs. road) and two comparisons (hits and outs), there is again $1 \times 1 = 1$ degree of freedom, and the obtained Chi-square again exceeds the critical value of 3.84 at 5 percent.

Chi-square may be generalized to more than two categories. For example, Boggs's batting averages for successive thirds of the season—early (April–May), middle (June–July), and late (August–September)—could be simultaneously compared. The expected number of hits is obtained in each case by multiplying the total at-bats in that category by .330. In this case, there are three categories (early, middle, and late), so there would be 2 degrees of freedom. An example of the complete calculations is presented in Appendix D.

Restrictions on Chi-square

Chi-square is actually a versatile statistic that has many uses. We shall encounter it again. However, its use is restricted to simple or unweighted proportions. For example, it cannot be used to compare slugging averages. Great care must be exercised in interpreting the results of these kinds of comparisons. The likelihood of any difference being a chance event is less than 5 percent, but one must be very careful that this is not one of those cases.

If Chi-square was computed on home-road differences for all players, about 5 percent of the values would be larger than the critical value, even in the absence of consistent home-road differences. It is not a good idea to assume that the differences between two situations for a player are significant without further evidence. Situational differences for a particular player often come and go or even reverse themselves from season to season. This usually does not occur because the player's sensitivity to the situational variable changes but because differences attributed to the situational variable are often simply chance occurrences.

All statistics carry some assumptions. In other words, the statistic requires that certain conditions be met or the rules of chance probability will not apply. The most important assumption in the case of chi-square is that each event included in the analysis is an independent event. In other words, what happens on one plate appearance is not affected by what happens on another. In most areas where chi-square is used, researchers are careful to collect data so that the condition of independence is met. Baseball data, however, must be taken for what they are. Whenever chi-square is used to evaluate a proportion or differences between a proportion, one must be prepared to assume independence. There are certain times when this assumption may be questioned. Later in the chapter we shall examine some situations where independence is unlikely.

Chi-square also carries some important restrictions. Chi-square is one of a class of statistics that are *estimation* statistics. In other words, you do not compute chi-square, just as you do not compute Var(E), the error variance. You simply estimate chi-square from the actual data. To be accurate, chi-square requires that expected values be larger than 5.

Chi-square also requires that every event be included in the analysis. In other words, it is based on an exhaustive and mutually exclusive categorization of events. If at-bats are being analyzed, the outs must be included for every at-bat to be included; if it is games, the analysis must include both wins and losses. One cannot compare the frequency of hits or wins alone.

Evaluating Situational Variables

In evaluating the general effect of a situational variable rather than the effect on a particular player, the comparison data will often be presented as two overall proportions. For example, the proportion of successful stolen bases on artificial turf was reported as .727, and the proportion of successes on dirt was .671.

At first glance, chi-square might seem an easy and simple way to determine whether this difference indicates a genuine superiority of turf over dirt or it could be a chance result. Given the number of attempts and successes in the two conditions, the computation of chi-square is a simple matter. In this case, however, the assumption of independence should be seriously questioned. Remember, independence means that the result of each attempted steal is unaffected by the result of *any other* attempt in the sample. When several attempts come from one player, those attempts are not independent because a particular player's success rate determines the rate of success of all of his attempts. One player who contributes disproportionally to the total could produce a significant effect all by himself despite the fact that he is the only one affected.

This leads to a very important restriction on the use of chi-square: It is widely accepted among statisticians that chi-square should not be used when various people (players) contribute more than one observation to the total proportion. Many situational statistics are in the form of overall percentages derived by combining the results for several players. An overall chi-square simply does not provide a legitimate assessment of differences in these cases. This precludes assessment of team statistics with chi-square because they also result from combinations of several plate appearances by each player.

The Legitimate Use of Chi-square

Because baseball and the computer provide so much data, it is easy to get confused by the wealth of numbers. There is a kind of warmth and security in a proportion based on 13,000 plate appearances, but if those 13,000 plate appearances do not provide a realistic indication of what was really happening, they are a waste of numbers. It is not necessary to use *all* of the data just because they are there. In fact, statistics are designed specifically to deal with small numbers of cases. Often, a small set of data allows inferences that are not possible with the larger set because the larger set is tainted or biased in some way or does not allow us to meet the assumptions of a statistical test.

There are two procedures for comparing overall proportions in the face of nonindependence. The necessary requirement, however, is that results be available for each player who contributed to the total.

The Contingency Test

Instead of taking the entire sample of data, it is possible to sample *one case at random* from each player under each condition. Proportions generated by this procedure may be legitimately compared by means of chi-square since each case within each condition is an independent measure.

Example: In comparing stolen-base success rate on artificial turf and on dirt, taking one attempt from each player on each type of surface would result in a successful steal or a failure (caught stealing) under each condition.*

The data used in this and the succeeding example were taken from The 1990 Stats Baseball Scoreboard, *published by Stats, Inc.*

There are four possible results for each player: success on both, success on dirt only, success on turf only, and failure on both. Each player's outcome could then be categorized to obtain the following table:

		Turf		
		Caught	Steal	Total
Grass:	Steal	9	29	38
	Caught	3	12	15
	Total	12	41	53

For example, 29 of the 53 players stole successfully on both surfaces; 3 of them were caught both times. The random selection process resulted in 41 of the 53 players stealing successfully in their one selected attempt on turf (77 percent) while 38 stole successfully on grass (72 percent). These are very close to the combined proportions based on all attempts.

The computation of chi-square may be simplified in this case. If we represent the four quantities in the table (9, 29, 3, and 12) as

$$A \quad B$$
$$C \quad D$$

chi-square is simply $([A-D]-1)^2 / (A+D)$ with 1 degree of freedom. (Note: $A-D$ must be positive. If $D>A$, then take $D-A$.) In this case, $(12-9-1)^2 / (12+9) = (3-1)^2 / 21 = 4/21 = .19$. The chi-square falls far below the level of chi-square (3.84) that occurs by chance 5 percent (or even 10 percent) of the time. From this analysis, there is little evidence to support the superiority of turf over dirt.

Note that we state the conclusion as "little evidence." The analysis does not provide a definitive answer to the question. It merely provides additional evidence. The strength of that evidence depends upon the size of chi-square; that is, how likely it is to have occurred by chance.

The Sign Test

If we examine the stolen-base data for the list of players, we find that 28 players had a higher rate (proportion) of success on turf than on grass, while the reverse was true for the remaining 25 players. If there are only chance differences between the two kinds of fields, then we would expect half of the players, 26.5, to perform better on dirt and the other half to perform better on turf.

Subtracting the observed frequencies from the expected gives values of +1.5 and −1.5. Squaring each of these values and dividing by the expected frequency of 26.5 gives two values that sum to a chi-square of 1.70. Again this is far below the criterion value needed to assume that there is any effect of surface on steals. In using the *sign test,* be sure to include *all* players, both positive and negative differences. The sign test always has 1 degree of freedom. It is called the sign test because the analysis is based on the number of differences in some specified (plus or minus) direction.*

The sign test does not require that the statistic being compared be a proportion. You could compare earned run averages, runs created, or any statistic that is computable from two samples of plate appearances for the same player. For example, you might compare the earned run averages at home and on the road for a group of pitchers. If there was no home-road difference, half of the pitchers would have a higher earned run average at home, and half would have a higher earned run average on the road. Again, the contribution to the total chi-square is the same for every player (either a + or a −) regardless of how many innings pitched were involved in the statistic.

These two forms of chi-square are perfectly legitimate. They meet all assumptions necessary for the use of chi-square. The critical aspect of the data is that each player contributes only one case to the frequencies being analyzed. Hence, each case is independent of the others. Neither statistic is very powerful in its ability to detect small differences unless those differences are constant from player to player.

A Special Use of Chi-square: Testing for Outliers

We have often pointed out that in a large sample of players 5 percent will differ from the average by 1.96 standard errors. These differences are in both directions, so that actually 2.5 percent would deviate from the average in one direction and 2.5 percent in the other. Equally true, we expect that 10 percent of the group will deviate from the average by 1.64 standard errors (5 percent each way). Knowing this, it becomes a fairly simple matter to determine whether deviations from some group average are more frequent than one would expect by chance.

Suppose you have a group of 200 players who played in a given season. For each player, you compute the difference between his career batting average and his batting average in that season and divide by the standard error for the season average, essentially converting that score into a z-score.

*Tied values (neither plus nor minus) are problematic for the sign test. One solution is simply to leave them out of the analysis. Another solution is to split them equally among the plus and minus categories. A third possibility is to place them all in the minus category. The logic of this maneuver is that usually the category labeled + is the one in which you are interested (positive cases). Therefore, + stands for positive cases and − for cases in which there was no positive difference. In the present example, we would be testing those players who are more successful in stealing bases on turf against those who are not.

The computation initially requires an estimate of the standard error for each player. This is not the standard deviation of the 200 batting averages but essentially the square root of Var(E). For a simple proportion, Var(E) for each player will be $P(1-P)/AB$, where P is estimated from the career proportion for that player.* *Example:* Based on a career value of .308, the standard error for 564 at-bats for Ashburn would be SQRT ([.308 × .692] / 564), or .019. Therefore, Ashburn's average of .266 would have a z value of (.308 − .266) / .019 = 2.21. Suppose we find that 20 players had z values larger than +1.64. On the basis of chance, we would expect 5 percent of the 200 players, or 10, to have z-scores above 1.64 (and another 10 to have values less than 1.64). The expected number of z-scores less than 1.64 is therefore 190. The computation of chi-square is carried out exactly as before:

$$\text{Above Criterion} = (20-10)^2/10 = 10^2/10 = 10.00$$
$$\text{Below Criterion} = (180-190)^2/190 = -10^2/190 = .53$$

In this case, chi-square was 10.53, which is larger than the critical value at 1 percent, 6.64. In that sample of 200 players, too many have z values above 1.64. We will find only 20 or more players with z larger than 1.64 less than 1 percent of the time by chance. We are therefore led to believe that some players are having "exceptional" years. The statistic does not tell us which ones are having those years "for real" and which are just lucky.

In fact, it is possible to define several criterion points in this way. Each one specifies the expected percentage of cases that would fall beyond that critical point based on chance. These are essentially the values given in Table 1, Appendix C. For example, 10 percent of the 200 (20 players) would be expected to have z greater than 1.28. Note that in the present example we used the 10 percent point rather than the more conventional 5 percent point to keep expected values at 10 or more.

Statistics that consist of weighted sums or proportions will require the more complex procedure described in Chapter 7 for obtaining SE of weighted sums.

14

Analysis of Variance

This chapter introduces some other procedures that may be used to evaluate situational effects. The goal of these procedures is to determine whether some situational factor produces a general effect on players' performance. For example, what is the effect of a home field, or even some particular home field, on the players who play there? What is the effect of artificial turf?

We have seen that a direct comparison of overall proportions by means of chi-square is not justified whenever each player contributes more than one plate appearance to the overall proportion. Some statistical procedures do not face this limitation. The procedure we will discuss here is actually a set of methods, known collectively as *analysis of variance* because they consist of partitioning the total variance into its various components.

We have already seen how this principle operates in determining reliability (Chapter 7). The reliability of a list of players ranked on some statistic was estimated by separating the variance (differences) among players into two components: that due to random error, Var(E), and that due to actual differences between players, Var(T). The procedures discussed here are an extension of the same logic to consider variance produced by situational factors.

The Logic of Analysis of Variance

Suppose you have three players from the Houston Astros who hit 6, 7, and 8 home runs, respectively, and another group of three players from the Chicago Cubs who hit 9, 10, and 11 home runs, respectively. It would appear that the Cub players are better home run hitters not just because the mean for the Cubs (10) was higher than the mean for the Astros (7) but because the worst Cub player hit more homers than the best Houston player. In other words, the difference between means for the two teams was larger than the differences between the players within a team.

127

Now consider two more sets of players. The Astros players had 1, 7, and 13 home runs, and the Cubs had 4, 10, and 16. The means for the two teams are still 7 and 10, but now there is some overlap. In fact, one Houston player hit more home runs than two of the three Cubs players. In this case, the differences between players *within* each team almost overshadows the difference between the means for the teams. If we are going to talk about a consistent difference between teams, the difference between the means of the two teams should be greater than the differences between individual players on each team.

The statistic we will use to compare conditions is essentially the ratio of the variance between means for different conditions to the variance among the players within each condition. It is called *F*.

$$F = \text{Var}(C) / \text{Var}(Pwc)$$

The ratio tells us whether the means (conditions) differ from one another more than we would expect by chance when the differences between players are considered.

Computational Procedure

There are different procedures for computing *F*, depending upon the composition of the data and the nature of the statistic. Unlike chi-square, the analysis-of-variance procedure may be used with any derived statistic. In Chapters 4 and 5, a distinction was made between additive and nonadditive statistics. Essentially, additive statistics consist of a sum or weighted sum of the events that take place on each at-bat, plate appearance, or batter faced. One procedure may be used with both additive and nonadditive statistics. A second procedure is suitable only for additive statistics.

In addition, there are two kinds of factors that may be studied. The first involves comparisons of separate groups of players who differ in some particular characteristic such as left-handed vs. right-handed batters or ground-ball vs. fly-ball hitters. These are called *separate-groups analyses* because the players in each condition are different players. The second type of analysis compares situations in which a statistic is obtained from each player under two conditions, such as facing left-handed vs. right-handed pitchers, home games vs. road games, or clutch vs. nonclutch situations. These are called *within-player analyses*.

This chapter presents computational examples and discusses the analysis for both additive and nonadditive statistics with both separate-groups and within-player analyses. The computational examples will be carried out on a very small set of players to make the computations easier to follow. Therefore, the results of the examples should not be taken seriously. Slugging average will serve as an example of an additive statistic, and production index (slugging average plus on-base average) will be used as an example of a nonadditive statistic. Ground-ball vs. fly-ball hitters will provide the situational factor for the separate-groups analysis, and batters facing left-handed vs. right-handed pitchers will be used to exemplify a within-player analysis.

The purpose of each analysis is to determine whether the situational factor produces a difference in average performance beyond that resulting from differences between players.

Case I: Separate-Groups Analysis

This is the simplest type of analysis of variance procedure and may be used with additive or nonadditive statistics. The table below provides the production ratio for five ground-ball hitters and five fly-ball hitters.* Values were multiplied by 1000 to eliminate the decimal.

Ground Ball	PrI	Fly Ball	PrI
Baines	819	Strawberry	879
Gwynn	772	Clark	805
Puckett	811	Davis	816
Walton	679	Bell	725
Thompson	620	Evans	740
Total	3701		3965

Overall Total = 7666

The principles for partitioning sums of squares is always the same and follows the procedure introduced in Chapter 7. To get a sum of squares, the sum for each condition is squared and divided by the number of values making up that sum; then each of those results is summed. A correction factor is subtracted from this total to yield the sum of squared deviations of the various means from the overall mean. The correction factor is computed by squaring the sum of all individual values, then dividing by the total number of values.

*A ground-ball batter is one who hits more than 1.5 ground balls for every fly ball. A fly-ball batter is one who hits fewer than one ground ball for every fly ball. The players were selected from a list appearing in the 1990 Stats Baseball Scoreboard. They were not selected at random but were chosen to make the "best" example. The data for batters facing left- and right-handed pitchers is from the 1990 Major League Handbook, also published by Stats, Inc.

The first value computed is the correction factor.

$$C = 7666^2 / 10 = 5,876,755.6$$

The sum of squared deviations between the two conditions is

$$SSc = 3701^2 / 5 + 3965^2 / 5 - C = 5,883,725.2 - C = 6969.6$$

The second component represents the deviations of the value for each of the players in a group from the mean of that group. It is the sum of squares between players within that group. For the ground-ball hitters,

$$SSpwg = 819^2 + 772^2 + \ldots - 3701^2 / 5 = 2,769,907 - 2,739,480.2 = 30,426.8$$

and for the fly-ball hitters,

$$SSpwf = 879^2 + 805^2 + \ldots - 3965^2 / 5 = 3,159,747 - 3,144,245 = 15,502$$

To get the variances, first SSc is divided by *1 less* than the number of sums that went into its computation—in this case, $2 - 1 = 1$.

$$Var(C) = 6969.6 / 1 = 6969.6$$

Var(P) is obtained by pooling the two within-condition components. First add the two sums of squares, then divide by the total number of players involved in the analysis minus the number of conditions $(10 - 2 = 8)$.

$$Var(Pwc) = (30,426 + 15,502) / 8 = 5741.1$$

The ratio of Var(C) to Var(Pwc) defines *F*. Therefore,

$$F = 6969.6 / 5741.1 = 1.21$$

Again, the logic of *F* in this case rests upon the variation between players. If the players vary more between one another than the means vary from one another, any differences between the means could be attributed to chance. The obtained *F* is evaluated from Table 3, Appendix C. The critical value of *F* depends upon the two denominators. First find the column for the denominator of Var(C), then appropriate row corresponding to the denominator of Var(Pwc). In column 1, row 2 (8), an *F* of 5.32 is necessary to conclude that the difference is due to more than chance.

The critical value of *F* is interpreted just like the critical value of chi-square. Values of *F* larger than 5.32 will occur less than 5 percent of the time by chance, given the variability between players. Therefore, based on this sample of players, there is little evidence that the ground-ball hitters differ consistently from fly-ball hitters in production index; that is, the difference is not significant. Generally speaking, a statistic is more powerful in finding differences with larger samples. A sample of 5 does not provide a very powerful test.

Case II: Within-Players Analysis

The rationale underlying F and the computational procedures differ somewhat when the same players provide a measure for both conditions. The data for the computational example consist of the production index for five right-handed batters batting against left-handed and right-handed pitching. Note that we have added a third column to the data; the sum of the two production index values for each player. This is not the overall production index but the actual sum of the two values.

Player	Left	Right	Total
Bell	840	767	1607
Clark	914	850	1764
Jacoby	766	726	1492
Randolph	741	666	1407
Wallach	858	722	1580
Totals	4119	3731	7850

We begin as usual by computing the sum of squares between left- and right-handed pitching based on the deviation of each condition from the overall average. This sum of squares is computed exactly as in the first example.

$$SSc = 4119^2 / 5 + 3731^2 / 5 - 7850^2 / 10 = 6,177,304.4 - 6,162,250 = 15,054.4$$

Because there are only two conditions, the variance based on this sum of squares is also 15,054.4. In this case, however, we do not want to compare the variance for conditions with the variance between players. Instead, we will look at a somewhat different aspect of the data.

Suppose we computed the difference in production ratio against left- and right-handed pitching for each player. If the effect of handedness was consistent, every player would show about the same improvement against southpaws; all the difference values would be the same. On the other hand, if some players performed better against lefties and others against righties, the effect of handedness would be inconsistent, and even a large difference in the average between the two kinds of pitching would be meaningless.

Large and inconsistent differences between players mean that there is an interaction between players and pitching. An *interaction* means that the effect of one factor depends upon something else. In this case, the effect of pitching depends upon which player you look at. If we are going to place any faith in an overall effect of handedness, the difference between left- and right-handed pitching summed over players should be greater than the interaction between pitching handedness and players.

The relevant value of *F* will therefore consist of a ratio between the variance for conditions (handedness) and the variance for the interaction between players and pitcher handedness. The table of data consists of rows (players) and columns (handedness). We have already computed a sum of squares for the difference between columns (SSc). We may also compute the sum of squares for differences between players (SSp) from the row totals as follows:

$$SSp = 1607^2 / 2 + 1764^2 / 2 \ldots - 7850^2 / 10 = 6,198,129 - 6,162,250 = 35,879$$

This computation is no different from that for any sum of squares. We take the value for a player, square it, divide by 2 because there are two values making up the player's total. The sum of squares is then obtained by summing these values for each player and subtracting C. It is also possible to compute a sum of squares for the deviation of each individual value from the overall mean. This total sum of squares (SSt) is the same as the total sum of squares used in computing the reliability.

$$SSt = 840^2 + 914^2 + \ldots + 722^2 - 7850^2 / 10 = 6,215,702 - 6,162,250 = 53,452$$

If you add the sums of squares for rows to the sum of squares for columns, it will be less than the total sum of squares. The remainder is the interaction.

$$SSint = SSt - SSc - SSp = 53,452 - 15,054.4 - 35,879 = 2518.6$$

We already have Var(C), so all that remains is to get Var(int). That is obtained by dividing SSint by the product of 1 less than the number of conditions (1) and 1 less than the number of players (4). Therefore,

$$Var(int) = 2518.6 / (4 \times 1) = 629.65$$

and

$$F = 15,054 / 629.65 = 23.91$$

Again, F is evaluated by finding the critical value in the first column and fourth row of Table 3, Appendix C. The critical value for F is 7.71. In other words, values larger than 7.71 will occur less than 1 percent of the time by chance. Since the obtained value exceeds that value, it provides evidence that right-handed batters do have a higher production ratio against left-handed pitchers than against right-handed pitchers.

Additive Statistics

For additive statistics, it is possible to carry out the analysis so that the means for players and conditions are weighted by the number of plate appearances, at-bats, batters faced, and so on, contributed by each player. Case I and II analyses do not do this. A player with few at-bats contributes as much to the analysis as one with many at-bats.

There is nothing inherently wrong with weighting each value the same, but there may be a considerable difference between the weighted and unweighted averages. When a choice is available, it should be carefully considered whether weighting the means is appropriate. Most baseball analysts prefer to deal with overall statistics (weighted averages) instead of unweighted means. Case III and IV analyses provide a procedure for doing this, and as we shall see, there are occasionally other advantages to be gained from these procedures.*

Case III: Separate-Groups Analysis

The analysis in this case is carried out on the frequencies of events composing the numerator (hits, total bases, etc.) rather than the statistic itself, and the various sums are weighted by the total plate appearances or at-bats in each case, but the basic procedure for computing variance components is the same.

Here are the at-bats and total bases for five ground-ball hitters and five fly-ball hitters:

*For those familiar with the analysis of variance model, the analyses consider at-bats or plate appearances to be nested within players and conditions. Players and at-bats (plate appearances) are considered random and conditions as fixed effects. Since plate appearances must be a random variable, the nesting effects are assumed to be zero, allowing the assessment of some variables that are confounded in nested designs in which the nested variables are fixed effects. If this does not make sense to you nonstatisticians, do not worry about it. It simply provides the technical rationale for using the form of analysis suggested here.

Ground Ball	AB	TB	Fly Ball	AB	TB
Baines	415	183	Strawberry	542	281
Gwynn	573	238	Clark	600	269
Puckett	551	246	Leonard	478	170
Boggs	619	259	Bell	562	237
Thompson	418	137	Evans	445	174
Totals	2576	1063		2627	1131

Overall AB = 5203
TB = 2194

The sum of squares for conditions is computed by squaring the sum of total bases for each condition (type of batter), then dividing each square by the total number of at-bats before subtracting C, the correction factor (overall total bases, squared, divided by the overall total at-bats).

$$C = 2194^2 / 5203 = 925.17$$
$$SSc = 1063^2 / 2576 + 1131^2 / 2627 - 925.17 = 438.65 + 486.93 - 925.17 = .41$$

The two sums of squares for the differences between players within each condition are similarly computed by dividing the square of each player's total bases by his at-bats, summing the values, and subtracting the sum for that condition, squared, divided by the total at-bats for the condition.

$$SSpwg = 183^2 / 415 + 238^2 / 573 \ldots - 1063^2 / 2576 = 442.66 - 438.65 = 4.01$$
$$SSpwf = 281^2 / 542 + 269^2 / 600 \ldots - 1131^2 / 2627 = 494.72 - 486.93 = 7.79$$

The variances Var(C) and Var(Pwc) are obtained exactly the same way as in Case I:

$$Var(C) = .41 / 1 = .41$$
$$Var(Pwc) = (4.01 + 7.79) / 8 = 1.475$$

In this case, Var(Pwc) is larger than Var(C). When this occurs, F is usually not even computed but is reported as less than 1.00. When there is no effect of the factor being evaluated, values of F that are larger than 1.00 will occur only about one-third of the time by chance. An F that is less than 1.00 is considered the ultimate statement of no effect.

Case IV: Within-Players Analysis

The rationale and computations are again an extension of Cases II and III. Here are the at-bats and total bases for the players in Case II against left-handed and right-handed pitching. Again the totals over all at-bats are required for each player.

	Left		Right		Total	
	AB	TB	AB	TB	AB	TB
Bell	178	92	435	189	613	281
Clark	125	55	330	154	455	209
Jacoby	152	75	367	141	519	216
Randolph	191	68	358	111	549	179
Wallach	160	80	413	160	573	240
Totals	806	370	1903	755	2709	1125

The variance values for computation of *F* are again Var(C) and Var(int). This time we will compute the total sum of squares first by squaring the total bases for each player in each condition, dividing by the appropriate at-bats, and subtracting the correction factor.

$$C = 1125^2 / 2709 = 467.19$$
$$SSt = 92^2 / 178 + 55^2 / 125 + \ldots + 160^2 / 413 - 467.19 = 477.54 - 467.19 = 10.35$$

The sum of squares for the difference between conditions is computed exactly as in Case III.

$$SSc = 370^2 / 806 + 755^2 / 1903 - 467.19 = 169.85 + 299.54 - 467.19 = 469.39 - 467.19 = 2.20$$

The sum of squares between players is

$$SSp = 281^2 / 613 + 209^2 / 455 \ldots - 467.19 = 473.59 - 467.19 = 6.40$$

and the interaction sum of squares is obtained by subtraction:

$$SSint = 10.35 - 2.20 - 6.40 = 1.75$$

The variances are obtained exactly as in Case II,

$$Var(C) = 2.20 / 1 = 2.20$$
$$Var(int) = 1.75 / 4 = .4375$$

and

$$F = 2.20 / .4375 = 5.03$$

From Table 3, we discover that the critical value for F at 5 percent is 7.71. Therefore values as large as 5.03 will occur *more* than 5 percent of the time by chance (actually, values larger than this occur about 8 percent of the time by chance). This illustrates one of the problems of significance tests. We are more or less left in limbo. If we want to keep our error rate at 5 percent, the value of F is too small. But there is little difference between 5 percent and 8 percent. Do we accept the error rate of 8 percent and conclude that the factor has an effect?

The best strategy when a value is close to the critical value is to withhold judgment. In this case, the number of players is quite small. Adding more players to the analysis would probably tip the scales one way or the other. You have to remember that the statistical test does not make the decision; it only provides evidence one way or another. A value of F that is significant at the 8 percent level may provide some evidence for the existence of a situational factor, but it is not strong evidence.

Evaluating the Interaction

In Case IV, the within-player analysis, the denominator of F consists of the interaction between players and conditions. It is possible to determine whether this interaction is significant by comparing it with the random variation in individual at-bats or plate appearances, our old friend unsystematic error variance, Var(E). In Chapter 8, we discussed certain situational factors that could produce a *constant* effect; that is, an effect that was the same for all players. The interaction variance, Var(int), reflects the degree to which players differ *unsystematically* between the two conditions being compared. This interaction could be due to unsystematic error, or it could be a result of the fact that the different conditions actually affect players differently.

In carrying out the Case IV analysis, it does not matter which is true. When comparing conditions, F is a valid statistic regardless of what is responsible for the interaction. Nevertheless, it is an interesting question in itself because the presence of an interaction effect tells us more about the effect of the situational factor being studied. If the interaction is just random error, the interaction variance, Var(int), will equal the variation due to random error, Var(E). If the situational factor produces systematic changes but these differ for various players, the interaction variance will be significantly larger than the error variance.

We already have computed the interaction variance, Var(int). All that remains is to compute the error variance, Var(E). The procedure used in Chapter 7 to measure reliability will provide a satisfactory estimate of Var(E).

This quantity then serves as the denominator for an F ratio in which Var(int) is the numerator.

$$F(\text{int}) = \text{Var(int)} / \text{Var(E)}$$

In this example, the general method suggested in Chapter 7 was used to obtain an estimate of Var(E) of .65. Therefore, the interaction between players and conditions in this Case IV example was

$$F = .4375 / .65$$

The critical value of F for these analyses is obtained from Table 3 from the column associated with the denominator for Var(int). The row is determined by the denominator used to convert SS(error) to Var(E). In most analyses, this value will be very large because the total number of at-bats is very large. The row will usually be the last one in the table. The critical value in this case is 2.37, but it matters not because F is less than 1.00. In other words, we have no evidence that the interaction is anything more than unsystematic (error) variation. The interaction in Case II analyses cannot be evaluated because the individual values for each at-bat or plate appearance are necessary to obtain an estimate of Var(E).*

Since it is often of considerable importance to evaluate the consistency of some situational effect from player to player, this particular analysis is quite valuable.

Extending the Analysis

It is also possible to generalize these procedures to two other kinds of situations. One involves the comparison of more than two groups of players or conditions. For example, we could investigate differences between players in three or four age groups or born in different states or with different amounts of minor league experience, and so on. The computational pro-

*Cases III and IV may appear appropriate for measures like the earned run average that are additive with respect to team totals. This is not the case, however. The procedure assumes that an individual measure exists for each unit in the denominator even though those measures are not involved in the calculations. Outs or innings are not a legitimate unit denominator in this respect because earned runs cannot be identified with a particular out. The appropriate procedure for these statistics is Case I or II. Cases III and IV are suitable for analyzing frequencies in single categories as well as weighted and unweighted proportions. They are also suitable for total offense or batting runs, even with stolen-base attempts included, because the individual values exist even if we do not know what they are. Unless those values are actually known, however, it is not possible to assess the contribution of Var(E) to the interaction in Cases III and IV.

cedures in this case are simple extensions of the two-group situation. Only a single value of F results from these analyses, which creates another problem of interpretation. With more than two conditions, a significant difference is nonspecific in the sense that it tells you that the conditions differ but does not tell you which ones differ from which. There are special procedures for diagnosing specific differences when an overall F indicates a difference involving more than two conditions, but these will not be covered here.

The second important way the F procedure may be generalized is to study two factors at the same time. For example, one could compare left- and right-handed batters or pitchers in two leagues or left- and right-handed batters who are either ground-ball or fly-ball hitters. These arrangements are called *factorial designs* because all possible combinations of the factors being studied are included.

Here is an example of one such design. With two factors—left- vs. right-handed batters, ground-ball vs. fly-ball hitters—there are four conditions: left-handed ground-ball hitters, right-handed ground-ball hitters, left-handed fly-ball hitters, and right-handed fly-ball hitters. The table below shows the sums for such an analysis, using the model of Case III with batting average. The totals and averages are arranged in a two-way table, the columns representing ground-ball vs. fly-ball hitters and the rows representing left- and right-handed batters.*

	Ground			Fly			Total		
	AB	H	Avg.	AB	H	Avg.	AB	H	Avg.
Left	2785	882	.317	2545	691	.272	5330	1573	.295
Right	2690	772	.287	2704	731	.270	5394	1503	.279
Total	5475	1654	.302	5249	1422	.271	10,724	3076	.287

The uniqueness of this arrangement is that it provides for a test for the *interaction* of the two factors. If you look at the batting averages for the four conditions, you will see a kind of asymmetry. For ground-ball batters, left-handers have a higher batting average than right-handers. For fly-ball batters, there is little difference due to handedness. This asymmetry defines the interaction. It says that the effect of one factor depends upon the other. In this case, the effect of handedness depends upon whether the player is a ground-ball or a fly-ball batter; being a left-handed batter is an advantage only if you hit lots of ground balls.

The analysis of the above data would produce three separate sums of squares in addition to the sum of squares between players within each

*The players in this analysis were selected from the 1990 Stats Baseball Scoreboard.

condition. Therefore, there would be three values of *F*. One value is based on the column "total" averages (.302 and .271), one on the row averages (.295 and .279), and one on the interaction (the relative difference between ground-ball and fly-ball batters, depending on whether they are left- or right-handed).

Interactions appear in two guises. The one illustrated here is a *divergent* interaction: A given factor has an effect for one group but not the other. The other interaction is a *cross-over* interaction: If left-handed batters did better when they hit ground balls and right-handed batters did better when they hit fly balls, there would be a crossover interaction. It is easy to see the difference graphically.

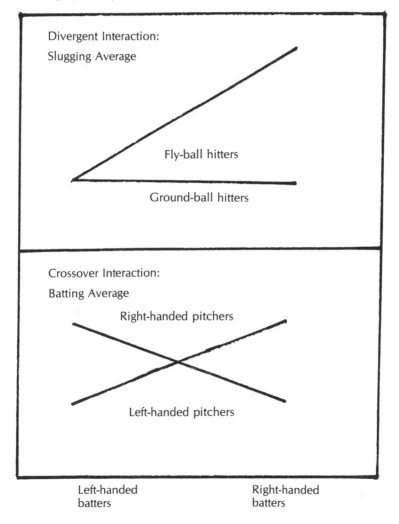

Entire books are devoted to analysis of variance procedures and arrangements. We have illustrated only four of the most basic types. Computational examples for a few other useful schemes are presented in Appendix D to enable the adventurous to extend their (and perhaps baseball's) horizons.

I would like to close this chapter with a bit of flag waving. Baseball analysts have largely ignored questions of statistical significance when discussing situational factors, just as they have ignored questions of reliability when discussing differences between players. The fact that many statistics are based on large numbers of at-bats or plate appearances does not in itself guarantee their reliability. The random error variance in most statistics is surprisingly large, and many situational effects are neither overwhelming nor consistent among players. Tests of significance ought to be routine whenever some situational effect is being discussed.

15

Sampling Problems

Baseball data do not exactly fit the mold for which statistical procedures were devised. The most important differences are those related to the selection of *samples* of players used in various analyses. There are two separate problems related to player selection. One problem relates to the generality of the results, the other to the validity of the results.

Generality

The purpose of comparing samples of players statistically is to apply the results from the particular group of players being examined to similar groups of players. If you found in 1989 that the mean batting average of all left-handed batters was different from the mean of all right-handed batters and you wanted to argue that this is not just a statistical anomaly that appeared in that sample of batters, not only is statistical evaluation of the reliability of that difference required, but some justification of its applicability to other groups of players is also necessary.

It then becomes a matter of whom that sample of batters represents. Statistically speaking, it is possible to generalize only from a sample to the population from which the sample was obtained. A *population* is the group from which the sample was selected. It may be defined as broadly or narrowly as you wish, but all members of the population must be eligible for the sample, and if generality is intended, the sample must be chosen in certain ways.

Any statistical analysis begins with a definition of the population—that group to which you wish the results to apply. Sometimes a population is defined by the at-bats, plate appearances, or batters faced for a particular player. Whatever you find, you are interested only in generalizing results to the past, present, or future at-bats and so on for that player. When you ask about the effect of some situational factor, you are interested in a population of players. That is, you want to say that a particular situational factor has an effect on some particular group of players. That population may be highly restricted.

All the players who had over 400 at-bats in 1942 and played for the St. Louis Browns are a population. Likewise, all the players who played in 1942 are a population, and all the players who have ever played are a population. The most interesting population of all consists of everyone who has ever played or ever will play. If we find that artificial turf produces a larger number of ground-ball singles than natural turf, we would like that result to be completely general, not restricted to a particular time, space, or set of players.

Now, obviously the set of players who contribute measures to the analysis is restricted, and statistically you can generalize only to that population from which the sample of players was obtained. If broad generalization is your goal, samples should be taken from as broad a range of players as possible. One would not do, as we have done throughout most of this book: restricting the sample to players from a couple of years. Statistical generalization in most of our examples would be restricted to 1989 or 1990, for that is where most of the examples came from.

Almost all reported analyses of baseball are carried out on data from the major leagues. Any generalizations that result from these analyses, no matter how large or broad the samples, are statistically restricted to major league baseball. There is nothing wrong with this procedure. It is simply the result of the way the population is defined, and that is the population most fans are interested in.

An ideal sample, however, is seldom obtainable. The best samples for discovering principles with broad application would require selecting players at random from some large data base such as *The Baseball Encyclopedia*. For some problems—for example, comparing left- and right-handed batters or players of different seasons or eras—this may be possible. For others, however, either some data are not available or the comparison is not relevant. Many situational statistics are not available except for the most recent years. The distinction between artificial turf and natural surface was not relevant until artificial surfaces became common. The distinction between indoor and outdoor baseball is feasible only for the last few years; the ratio of day games to night games shifted dramatically after World War II. The list goes on and on.

Faced with such dilemmas, the researcher often resorts to "common sense" rather than statistical generality. Generality is argued not just on the representative nature of the sample but whether there is any reason to expect a difference between the population from which the sample was obtained and similar populations. If an interaction between handedness and ground-ball vs. fly-ball hitting is found in 1989, does this mean that it always has been and always will be so? You could make a pretty good argument for generality in this case because there is nothing immediately apparent in the changes that have taken place over the years that would lead you to think otherwise. The bottom line, however, is that the burden of proof must eventually be more than rational. The data will out, and generality is often a matter of showing that the same results will be obtained when sampling from a different population. The more often a particular difference appears with different samples, the more confidence we have in its generality.

Validity

When a difference between two or more samples is shown to be an unlikely consequence of random sampling, that result is statistically valid. Determining what produced that difference is another issue entirely.

If two samples are chosen at random from two populations, a difference can be attributed to anything that makes those populations differ, but differences are not always what they appear to be. Baseball is full of self-fulfilling prophecies. If pitchers believe that they must keep their pitches low to get batters out (whether it is true or not), then good low-ball hitters will predominate. If it is widely believed that bases are easier to steal on artificial turf, teams whose home field is artificial are not only more likely to try to steal but may even load up on players that are good base stealers. A player who has a reputation of not being able to hit left-handed pitching, deserved or not, gets very few at-bats against left-handed pitching, and if he does, it may not be against the "quality" left-handers.

Some of these factors may have a profound effect on samples, hence on the results of some comparisons. Changes in playing conditions can affect not only play but the players who are selected to play. Some of these "population changes" are obvious. The designated hitter makes room for poor-fielding sluggers who before were a liability, but a more subtle effect may also occur. Teams no longer burdened with a .150-hitting pitcher can afford a .198-hitting shortstop or even a .215-hitting center fielder if he can catch and throw the ball reliably. In 1954, the poorest hitter among the regulars had a batting average of .225. In 1990, a batting average of .225 was barely 1 standard deviation below the mean.

Selective sampling effects may also produce apparent differences where none exist. Suppose turf teams not only load up on better base stealers but attempt to steal more frequently because of it. Since they play more games on turf, the overall success rate on turf will be inflated because their attempts contribute more to the total on turf than those of their slower counterparts who play on turf less frequently. In a similar vein, when a left-handed batter has a reputation of not being able to hit left-handed pitching, he gets few at-bats against that pitching. Therefore, he will contribute less to the total than a left-handed player who is successful against left-handed pitching. The result is that the overall success rate of left-handed hitters against southpaw pitching could be overestimated.

As has often been pointed out, a ballpark believed to be a launching pad often results in more at-bats for boomers and fewer for the scratch-and-scramblers because of managerial decisions about whom to play. Likewise, the scramblers may be seduced into going for the downs more often. The result would be a dramatic park effect on home runs, whether the park has anything to do with it or not.

One must be very careful when interpreting the results based on samples to take into account these and other subtle sample biases that may contribute to or detract from differences assumed to be produced by the factors of real interest. Just because some explanation of a statistical comparison result seems reasonable does not ensure its validity.

Summary

Validity in a comparison is not indicated by statistical significance but can be obtained only by carefully isolating the conditions responsible for the effect. Often this may require a series of well-reasoned comparisons of several different kinds before it is clear what is responsible for a difference.

Actually, significance is more like reliability. Whether it is a difference between players or between conditions, significance means that a difference is not likely to be due to chance. That is all it means. In a more concrete sense, it means that a difference is predictable, that it will usually occur whenever the conditions are the same.

If Wade Boggs has a significantly better *true* batting average than Kirby Puckett, it means that his actual average will exceed Puckett's average on most if not all occasions. If stealing bases is significantly easier on artificial turf than on natural surface, in most comparisons this should be apparent. In dealing with statistical significance, the bottom line is always *replicability*. A real difference will reappear again and again when given the chance. A bogus difference will come and go. Statistical significance tells us which differences are likely to be consistent and which are not and is most useful when predictions are in order.

Once again, however, significance does not ensure that the difference is due to what you think it is. Boggs may not be a better hitter than Puckett but may have an advantage in his home park and/or the pitchers he faces during a season. Artificial turf may not in itself produce a higher success rate for stolen bases but may result from better base stealers playing more games on artificial turf. A statistical difference may result from *anything* that makes the samples different.

16

Strategy

One of the most fascinating applications of statistical theory to baseball is the evaluation of managerial strategy. There are two classes of strategies: lineup and playing.

Lineup strategies involve the movement of players into and out of the game—constructing the batting order, selecting and changing pitchers, offensive and defensive substitutions, and so on. These strategies often involve considerations that are not entirely based on winning individual games (e.g., giving the bench or bullpen playing time, resting a veteran regular, or trying out a rookie). They will not be considered here except in passing.

Playing strategies are of several kinds: batting strategies, such as sacrifice bunt and hit-and-run; base-running strategies, such as stolen bases, taking extra bases on hits, and advancing on outs; defensive strategies, such as positioning players, pitchouts, and throws to hold the runner.

It is not the job of the statistician to tell the manager what to do. We have emphasized that statistics are ill-equipped to deal with specific instances. All that statistics can accomplish is to provide evidence on the long-term consequences of various actions. In principle, choice should be simple: Offensive strategy is dictated by maximizing runs scored, and defensive strategy is dictated by minimizing runs allowed. Although strategy is necessarily based on a total game, series, or season, actual strategic decisions, with the exception of starting lineup, are situational; they take place on particular plate appearances and under specific circumstances. We are going to examine one procedure for assessing the various courses of action in those circumstances.

Bases-Outs Tables and Run Potential

The basic tool for evaluating situational strategies is the *bases-outs table*. This table lists the average number of runs scored, given a particular constellation of runners on base and outs. Several tables have been published. They are *empirical* in that they represent actual results of games rather than speculations. One such table was used in the construction of the batting runs statistics.*

Average Number of Runs Scored

	Outs		
Runners	0	1	2
none	.45	.25	.10
First	.78	.48	.21
Second	1.07	.70	.35
Third	1.28	.90	.38
1 and 2	1.38	.89	.46
1 and 3	1.64	1.09	.49
2 and 3	1.95	1.37	.66
Full	2.25	1.55	.80

These values are *not* proportions or probabilities but average (mean) runs scored. For example, with a runner on first and none out, an average of .78 runs will score; with a runner on third and two out, an average of .38 runs will score.

The probability of numbers of runs scored may be derived directly from this table. The run potential for any combination is based on the contribution of the runners on base and that of the batter and all future batters. Suppose there is a runner on third with none out. A total of 1.28 runs would be expected. Of that total, the batter and any subsequent batters would contribute .45, which is the number of runs that should score with no one on base. Therefore, the runner on third would contribute the remainder, or $1.28 - .45 = .83$ runs. The latter figure, therefore, represents the probability that he will score. (Out of 100 players in this situation, 83 would be expected to score.) Likewise, with one out, the probability of scoring from third is $.90 - .25 = .65$, and with two outs the probability is $.38 - .10 = .28$.

One could compute the probabilities of scoring from second base with 0, 1, or 2 outs in the same manner, resulting in the following table:

Probability of Scoring

	Outs		
	0	1	2
Batter(s)	.45	.25	.10
Runner on First	.33	.23	.11
Runner on Second	.62	.45	.25
Runner on Third	.83	.65	.28

The values in this table are the ones derived by Palmer and published in Palmer and Thorn, The Hidden Game of Baseball.

If there is more than one runner on base, the separate probabilities may be combined to yield a single value. There are two rules for combining probabilities.

1. The *joint-occurrence rule:* If two events are independent (the occurrence of one event has no effect on the occurrence of the other), the probability that they will both occur is equal to the product of their separate probabilities:

$$\text{Pr A and B} = \text{Pr A} \times \text{Pr B}$$

2. The *either-or rule:* The probability that either of two events will occur is equal to the sum of the two probabilities, minus the probability of their joint occurrence (their product). If the two events are mutually exclusive, the probability of joint occurrence is zero.

$$\text{Pr A or B} = \text{Pr A} + \text{Pr B} - \text{Pr A and B}$$

Now let us see how these rules apply to combinations of bases-outs. Suppose we have runners on first and second with none out. The probability that the lead runner will score is .62, the probability that the trailing runner will score is .33, and the probability that the batter will score is .45. To compute the probability that both runners will score, we use the joint-occurrence rule. The probability is $.62 \times .33 = .20$.

This is not the probability of scoring two runs, however, since it does not take into account the possible fate of the batter. Two runs may score in several ways. The two runners may score and future batters not score, or one of the two runners may score and future batters not score, or one of the two runners may score along with a future batter.

There are three separate probabilities. First, the probability that both runners will score and a batter not score is $.62 \times .33 \times (1 - .45) = .11$. The probability that a batter will score and the runner on second will not is $.45 \times .33 \times (1 - .62) = .06$. And the probability that a batter and the runner on second will score is $.45 \times .62 \times (1 - .33) = .19$.

Using the either-or rule, the probability of scoring exactly two runs is the sum of all these probabilities ($.11 + .06 + .19 = .36$). In this case, we need not subtract the products because the three alternatives are *mutually exclusive;* only one of them can occur. Using this procedure, it is possible to compute the probability of scoring 0 to x runs given any bases-out situation.

Maximizing Run Potential

This is but part of the problem in evaluating a strategy. Unless the offensive manager is playing for a single run, any strategic maneuver should be designed to *increase* the run potential as much as possible. Every plate appearance begins with a run potential. When that plate appearance is concluded, there is a new run potential. The best strategies (or nonstrategies, like "hit away") is the one that maximizes the positive difference between the run potential at the start and that at the end of that player's plate appearance.

Statistically, the evaluation of outcomes is straightforward. Suppose there is a runner on first and no one out. As it stands, the average run potential is .78. After the next batter finishes his plate appearance, there are eight possible new bases-outs situations, each with its payoff in potential runs scored.

Average Number of Runs Scored: Remaining

Runners	Outs 0	1	2
none	.45#	—	.10
First	.78	.48	—
Second	1.07	.70	—
Third	1.28	.90	—
1 and 2	1.38	—	—
1 and 3	1.64	—	—
2 and 3	1.95	—	—
Full	—	—	—

In the table, those situations marked by dashes are not possible. For example, a batter coming to the plate with a runner on first and no outs cannot leave with a runner still on first base and two outs. Values marked by # means that runs have actually scored. In other words, the batter may hit a home run (thereby clearing the bases and scoring two runs) but leaves the situation at none on and none out: run potential = .45. Among the legitimate possibilities, he may advance the runner to second on an out (intentional or not), thus leaving the situation with a run potential of .70, or he may single the runner to third, leaving runners on first and third with none out and a run potential of 1.64.

The possible net gain or loss from that player's plate appearance can be obtained by subtracting .78 from the value of each possible outcome. If the runner or batter scores (as in the first four rows of column 1, no outs), we add a value of 1 or 2 to reflect the fact that runs are actually in the bank. The rewritten table would look like this:

Average Gain or Loss in Runs Scored for Each Situation

Runners	Outs		
	0	1	2
none	1.67	—	−.68
First	1.00	−.30	—
Second	1.29	−.08	—
Third	1.50	.12	—
1 and 2	.60	—	—
1 and 3	.86	—	—
2 and 3	1.17	—	—
Full	—	—	—

This table does not dictate any particular strategy, but it does point out that the only gain from an out requires the runner to go from first to third. A successful sacrifice bunt actually lowers the potential runs by .08. An unplanned out that advances the runner has the same effect. But an unsuccessful sacrifice or an out that does not advance the runner lowers the potential by .30 runs.

To evaluate the outcome in a particular situation, the run values must be multiplied by the probability that the result in each cell will occur. Suppose the batter will single the runner to third on 20 percent of his plate appearances. This will give him $.20 \times .86 = .172$ runs. Suppose further that on the remailing 80 percent of his plate appearances he makes an out that fails to advance the runner. Each of those outs has a value of −.30, so those plate appearances are worth $.80 \times -.30 = -.240$ runs. By adding up the results of each outcome, we obtain the total potential change that will result from that plate appearance. In this case, $.172 - .240 = -.068$. This means that an evaluation of possible strategies requires a consideration of the relative skills of both batter and runner.

Now let us take a more complete example. To simplify the situation, assume that the runner is a slug and that no pinch runner is available. In other words, the runner will not take any extra bases. The batter has the following record of proportion of times he produces various outcomes:

Single (or safe on error) = .178
Doubles = .012
Triples = .001
Home runs: .021

Walks = .011
Strikeouts = .128
Ground ball outs: .379
Other Outs: .270

We will assume, moreover, that 60 percent of the ground balls will result in double plays and that 5 percent will advance the runner. The remainder are force plays at second.*

We can now create another table by multiplying the runs gained in each outcome by the probability that the outcome will occur. If a situation can result in more than one outcome, the separate values are summed. For example, the probability that he will hit a home run is .021. Multiplying this value by the payoff in runs, 1.67, gives a value of .035 for the first cell (none on, none out). He can advance a runner to second base by a single or a walk. Therefore, that entry is $(.178 \times .60) + (.011 \times .60) = .113$.

Average Gain or Loss in Runs Scored Times
Probability of Occurrence

Runners	0	1	2
none	.035	—	−.154
First	.000	−.159	—
Second	.000	−.002	—
Third	.001	.000	—
1 and 2	.113	—	—
1 and 3	.000	—	—
2 and 3	.014	—	—
Full	—	—	—

These values allow a somewhat different evaluation. The total run potential for that batter is equal to the sum of all of the possible individual run potentials. If the batter is left to his own devices and performs up to snuff, the total change in run potential is −.152 runs. This means that in the long run if we let this batter hit away when he comes to bat with a runner on first, he will reduce our run-scoring potential by −.152 runs.†

Now suppose the manager asks the batter to sacrifice. The probabilities change considerably. The consequences of a bunt are (1) sacrifice out, (2) out with no advance or force out, (3) double play, (4) batter reaches base.

*Any manager worth his salary will have such data for his players and others in the league. As fans, however, we will usually have to guess at the actual probabilities.

†The fact that this is negative should not bother you. You have to realize that batters fail to come through almost 75 percent of the time on average. The usual result with men on base is to leave them there.

Suppose we estimate the probability of a successful sacrifice to be .500, a failed sacrifice .490, and double plays and reaching base each .05. Now, multiplying the payoff of each outcome by the probability of that outcome, the gain-loss table would look like this:

Runners	0	1	2
none	—	—	−.034
First	—	−.147	—
Second	—	−.040	—
Third	—	—	—
1 and 2	.030	—	—
1 and 3	—	—	—
2 and 3	—	—	—
Full	—	—	—

Average Gain or Loss in Runs Scored

The total value (sum) of these outcomes is an average of −.191 runs. A sacrifice is also a negative strategy and is "more negative" than letting the batter hit away.

Obviously, the key to this entire enterprise lies in an accurate assessment of the probabilities of various events. The ultimate result depends considerably on what is likely to happen. For example, a pitcher left to hit away with a runner on base will almost always add an out without advancing the runner. A bunt reduces this loss in the long run by moving the runner, even if it is successful only a small percentage of the time.

Of course, the manager may also wish to take the particular skills of the *next* batter into account. For example, if he is a low-average home run hitter, a sacrifice might not look as enticing as taking the chance on the fortunes of the present batter. Looking ahead this way would entail the construction of several other tables—the next batter, one for each possible outcome of the present batter. This sort of thing can get complicated in a hurry, and you can see why the manager might request a computer in his dugout. It is no wonder that managers often operate on hunches (subjective estimates of run potential).

The Break-Even Point

The assessment of any strategy begins with the assumption of "let it be." Any maneuver must be compared with what would happen if the normal course of events unfolded with no managerial intervention. This reference level might be called the *break-even point.*

In the above example, the break-even point would be −.152 runs. A sacrifice makes the situation worse, but we assumed that a sacrifice was successful only 50 percent of the time. Is there some level of success in which the loss would be less than .152 runs? The answer in this case is yes, and it is easy to see why.

Every successful sacrifice costs −.08 runs. If the success rate was 100 percent, the loss in run potential would be −.080, which is still negative but less than the loss of −.152 produced by hitting away. A player whose hit-away value is more positive than −.080, even if he was certain to advance the runner on a sacrifice, is likely to leave the inning in better shape if he hits away.

What success rate for sacrifices is necessary for our mythical batter to break even by sacrificing? If we keep the probability of reaching base and bunting into a double play at .05 each, this value may be obtained by solving the equation $.08X - .30 (.99 - X) = -.152$ for X:

$$\text{Point of Equality (X)} = (.297 - .152) / .22 = .66$$

In other words, if the probability of a successful sacrifice equals .66, he is likely to change the run potential by sacrificing the same amount as he would by hitting away. If the sacrifice success rate exceeds .66, a sacrifice will still have a negative value for this player, but it will be "less negative" than −.152. It is easy to see why this is the case. A poor batter stands a very good chance of making an out that does not advance the runner, which is more costly than an out that does advance the runner. Sacrificing changes this ratio favorably.

Each strategy must be evaluated with respect to a particular batter and situation. Whenever the sum of the values for the outcomes of some strategy yields greater gains (or less loss) than hitting away, that should be the more viable strategy.

Base-Running Strategies

In the above example, we used the batter's plate appearance as a reference. The runner might try to steal, which does not involve the batter. For a stolen base, only a few alternatives are possible. Starting again with no outs and a runner on first, the run potential is .78. The only things that can happen on a steal attempt are success and failure. A steal leaves the situation at 1.07 runs, a gain of .29 runs. A failure leaves it at .25, a loss of .53 runs. The break-even point is obviously zero (no change will occur if nothing is attempted). How successful will a runner have to be to break even? This may be rather easily computed from the original table as follows:

Point of equality = (Start Value − Failure Value) / (Success Value − Failure Value)

In this example,

Point of Equality = (.78 − .25) / (1.07 − .25) = .53 / .82 = .646

In other words, if the probability of a successful steal equals .646, you will break even. For steal success rates above .646, an attempted steal will gain runs; for values below .646, it will lose runs. This is true regardless of the batter's proficiency. One should note, however, that the actual consequences of an inning are cumulative, and the cost-payoff of the inning again depends upon the skills of the following batters as well as the immediate gain in run potential. It does not make sense to steal with the pitcher at bat, for a variety of reasons.*

Scoring a Single Run

When the inning is played to maximize the chances of scoring a particular runner rather than maximize total run production, the computations are similar. The first step is to translate the probabilities into gains (or losses) for that runner. For example, the probability that a runner on first base with none out will score is .33. Subtracting this value from the probability *for that runner* following various actions by the batter results in a table of gains and losses in probability.

Probability of Scoring			
	0	1	2
Runner Eliminated	.67#	—	−.23
Runner on First	—	−.10	—
Runner on Second	.29	.13	—
Runner on Third	.50	—	—

As in the previous example, these are "payoffs" and must be multiplied by the probability that the particular transition will occur:

---

*The 65 percent point of equality for steals of second base is true on average but in specific cases is misleading. To evaluate the stolen base in any specific situation properly, one would compare the sum of possible changes in run potential produced by the batter, multiplied by the probability of a successful steal with that resulting from an unsuccessful steal. If the failure results in the third out, the appropriate comparison value would be the run potential of the batter if he leads off the next inning.

Probability of Scoring

	0	1	2
Runner Eliminated	.014	—	−.052
Runner on First	—	−.053	—
Runner on Second	.055	.002	—
Runner on Third	.006	—	—

Summing the values as before, we find that the hit-away potential is −.028. Essentially, this means that the probability of scoring has dropped from .330 to .302.

Similarly, a matrix may be created for the sacrifice (or any other strategy) and multiplied by the appropriate probabilities (.500 was again used as the success rate for the sacrifice in this example).

Probability of Scoring

	0	1	2
Batter	—	—	−.012
Runner on First	—	−.049	—
Runner on Second	.015	.065	—
Runner on Third	—	—	—

The "sacrifice table" has a summed value of .019, which translates to a probability of .349. In other words, even a success rate of 50 percent increases the probability of scoring the runner from first, by about 2 percent over the break-even rate determined from the likely outcomes of hitting away. This illustrates an important point about the bases-outs tables. Maximizing the probability of scoring a single run and maximizing total potential runs are not the same game.

Other contingency tables may be used. For example, Thorn and Palmer, in *The Hidden Game of Baseball,* derive a table for the probability of winning a game, given a certain bases-outs value, after the seventh inning. The computation of strategies follows the same principles.

Lineup Strategies

We will not belabor these procedures further. Substitution strategies are fairly easy to evaluate. They simply change the probabilities of various outcomes that will multiply the payoff values in run potential. This is true whether it is a pinch hitter, a relief pitcher, or a defensive substitute. In principle, the exact long-term consequences of these changes could also be calculated.

Choice of starting lineup and batting order is an immensely complicated decision-making process. At present, there seem to be no relatively simple statistical procedures for dealing with this problem.

A Final Note

Statistical success of particular strategies refers to the long-term outcomes, not the result in a particular situation. If Jim Leyland is faced with Redus on first base, Bell at bat, and Van Slyke coming up, whether he opts for a sacrifice bunt from Bell may be a matter of comparing the run potential for sacrifice and hit away. Even if the situation is favorable for a bunt, all Leyland knows statistically is that if he always bunts in that situation, he will maximize his run production in the long run. Over the short run, even for an entire season, the strategy may fail to yield its expected results. Theoretically, there is a standard error for run potential, just as for any other statistically based measure. In the final analysis, however, the maximal strategy will eventually win out.

17

Potpourri

This chapter has no unifying theme but introduces a miscellaneous set of analytic procedures that describe a player's performance from a somewhat different angle. None of them have been extensively used, and all are relatively undeveloped and untested. Most require data beyond the traditional batting, pitching, and fielding categories, and some require information not recorded on the standard scoresheet.

Uses of Bases-Outs to Evaluate Players

The bases-outs table may be used to evaluate both batter and pitcher performance, but play-by-play data are required in both instances. In concept, it is simple, but in practice it is extremely complicated and except for small sets of games such as a World Series, requires the use of a computer.

The logic is as follows: A player comes to bat with a certain run potential value determined by the bases-outs situation at the time. He finishes his plate appearance with the run potential changed. For any given plate appearance, he is credited with the difference in run potential that results from that plate appearance plus whatever he does on the bases.

Example: An inning begins with a run value of .45. Knoblauch walks to start the inning, which leaves the value at .78. Knoblauch therefore receives credit for .78 − .45 = .33. Puckett comes to bat and singles, sending Knoblauch to second. The situation is now runners on first and second, no out (value = 1.38). The difference due to Puckett's action was 1.38 − .78 = .60. Puckett then gets picked off first, leaving only a runner at second with one out (value = .70). The cost of this negligence was 1.38 − .70 = .68. This is deducted from Puckett's total, to leave him with a value of − .08 for that plate appearance. Hrbek then walks, putting runners on first and second with one out (value = .89). Hrbek's contribution was therefore .89 − .70 = .19. Davis then grounds into a double play to end the inning. This little endeavor cost

157

Davis the .89 runs that existed when he came to bat. The result of the inning: Knoblauch .33, Puckett −.08, Hrbek .19, and Davis −.89. The run value (the sum of these values, including the .45 that started the inning) was zero (no runs scored). Summing a player's values over an entire game provides a measure of *runs produced*. The sum over all innings will equal the runs scored.

The system is not simple to use and is highly situation-dependent; the credit a batter receives for a given offensive act depends heavily on the circumstances surrounding his plate appearances, and those circumstances are not his doing. It has the advantage of measuring the *actual* contribution to run scoring, giving some credit to batters that move runners when they make outs and discrediting batters that leave runners on base at the end of an inning.

However, there are a number of arbitrary decisions that must be made when runners advance or are put out on bases. When a runner goes from first to third on a single, is the extra base credited to the batter or the runner? When a runner is picked off base on a line drive, did the batter hit into a double play, or was it bad base running? These sorts of problems must be left to the scorer's judgment unless arbitrary rules are formulated.

Doug Bennion has suggested a similar procedure that uses bases-outs values as a panacea for the inequities in assignment of runs and earned runs to pitchers. The principle is the same as that for batters. While a pitcher is in the game, all runs scored are credited to him. When he leaves the game in midinning, he leaves a particular bases-outs situation. He is charged with that value of that situation regardless of what happens to those runners. For example, Welch allows two runs in the first seven innings and is relieved in the eighth inning with one out and runners on second and third. The run potential value of this situation is 1.37, so Welch leaves the game having allowed 3.37 runs.

The relief pitcher inherits the run potential existing when he enters the game. He is then charged for all runs that score while he is pitching. For example, Eckersley comes in to pitch and has inherited 1.37 potential runs from Welch. If none of the runs score, he is credited with 1.37 runs (1.37 is subtracted from his total runs allowed for the season), but he is charged for any runs that score while he is pitching. If one run scores, his credit is reduced to .37. If both runs score, it becomes −.63.

Note that if none score, the 1.37 added to Welch's total and the 1.37 subtracted from Eckersley's total will keep the team total correctly balanced. While this rather elegant procedure does eliminate the correlation between a pitcher's record and the effectiveness of his bullpen, it does not eliminate the bias favoring relievers, who still need not get three outs to reset the bases-outs to zero.

Bennion also suggests that bases-outs be used to determine more equitably earned runs as opposed to unearned runs. When an error is made, simply compute the change in bases-outs value that results from the error and subtract that from the runs allowed. A one-out error that allows a run to score from third results in a run (value = 1), and it puts a runner on first with one out (value = .48). Thus the error was worth 1.48 runs.

The situation should have been two outs and a runner on third, a run value of .38. Thus the total "cost" to the pitcher was 1.48 − .38 = 1.10 unearned runs. This value is then deducted from the actual scoring, leaving him with a runner on first with one out and a credit so far of .10 unearned runs. If he pitches out of the inning, the credit remains. If the runner on first scores, it costs him 1 − .10 = .90 earned runs. In this case, a pitcher could give up fewer runs than unearned runs in any inning.

A simpler procedure might be simply to drop the extra .10 runs if the runner does not score but charge him with the .90 if he does score. This would keep the totals in balance. The value of any run that is unearned would then depend on the portion contributed by the error. At this point, the basis for any corrections of this kind is bound to be arguable, and other procedures based on the same principle are possible.

There is no reason why fielders could not be evaluated in terms of the run-potential consequences of their errors. If an error does not lead to a run scored, it may have little effect on the outcome of the game, but a two-out error that allows two runs to score may be devastating. Fielders as well as pitchers might be credited with the unearned portion of runs actually scored — the difference between what should have happened and what actually did.

The use of bases-outs is admittedly complicated. Whether it is worth the effort will depend upon whether such measures are able to provide information about players' performance that is not available from traditional categories.

Sequential Analyses

Most baseball statistics simply deal with the total number of events, not the order in which they occur. The following procedures provide possible procedures for evaluating sequences.

The Running Average

It is often of interest to examine the course of a player's performance during the season. Weekly summaries printed in many newspapers provide cumulative records, varying in detail as the season progresses. Cumulative summaries, however, reflect the player's total performance to that time and are highly variable early in the season. As the plate appearances pile up, changes in the performance from day to day and week to week are less likely to affect the cumulative total.

It is possible, of course, to simply "decumulate" these statistics. One could examine the weekly results by subtracting the cumulative totals from the week before from the current week's totals. Totals may also be obtained for larger time units, such as months.

There is another procedure that may be of some value in identifying peaks and valleys of player performance during the season. It is called the *running average*. After two weeks of play, or about 15 games, a regular player will have about 50 at-bats. Any statistic of interest (batting average, slugging average, etc.) may be computed for those plate appearances. From that point until the season is completed, simply add in the result of the next game, remove the result of the earliest game in the sequence, and recompute the statistic.

Suppose you decide to use 15-game sequences. After cumulating results for 15 games and computing the statistic of interest, you add in the results of his sixteenth game and drop the results from the first game. Then add in the seventeenth game and drop the second and so on. This maintains the number of games for each successive computation at 15 and the plate appearances at about 50 for each successive value. Since you are simply "replacing" one day's activity with another, changes from day to day will not be very dramatic, but any prolonged slump or hot streak will be reflected in a gradual rise or fall over several days.

Example: In the first 15 games, a player has 21 hits in 59 at-bats, for a batting average of .356. The next game, he goes 1 for 4, to total 22 hits in 63 at-bats. In the first game of the original 15, he had 3 hits in 4 trips. Subtracting this from the previous sum leaves 19 hits in 59 at-bats. The average for games 2–16 is .322. He then had an 0-for-4 day in game 17, replacing a 2-for-6 effort in game 2, leaving his running average at 17 / 57 = .298 for games 3–17. The entire season may be carried through this way. If the player was in 155 games, the final value is for games 141–155.

The advantage of this procedure is that the considerable day-to-day variability in performance does not obscure any regular changes that occur and that each statistic is based on about the same number of at-bats. An example of a running average is shown in the figure on the next page. The data are for Alvin Davis's batting average in 1986 for successive running sets of 15 games.*

---

*This could also be carried out one plate appearance at a time. It would provide a good indica-
tion of how inconsistent a player's performance is from at-bat to at-bat, but the graph would

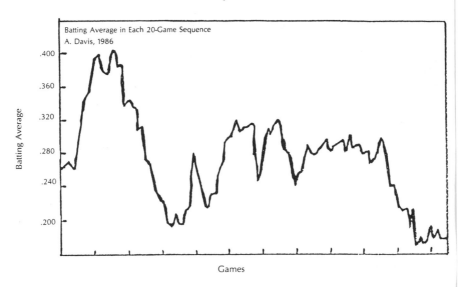

Batting Average in Each 20-Game Sequence
A. Davis, 1986

The Sequence of Events

A consistent batter will spread his hits, home runs, or what-have-you more or less equally over his plate appearances during a season, while a streaky player will get his in bunches. One way of measuring this effect is to look at the overall sequence of events. For example, every offensive event is separated by anywhere from 0 to *n* plate appearances in which that event does not occur.

Here is an example of a sequence of outs (O) and reaching base safely (B), separated into "runs" of various lengths.

BB OO BB OOOOO B OOOOOOO BB OOO B O BB O BBBBB O B
OOOO B OOOOO B OO B OOOO

There are 54 plate appearances. The player reached base 19 times and made outs 35 times. There are 22 "runs" (strings of the same event), starting with a run of reaching base twice in a row and ending with a run of four consecutive outs. In random arrangement of two events we would expect the average number of runs to be

$$\text{Mean Runs} = 1 + (2 \times O \times B) / (O + B)$$
$$\text{Mean Runs} = 1 + (2 \times 35 \times 19 / 54) = 25.6 \text{ runs}$$

(continued): show considerable irregularity. Keeping at-bats constant at 50, each hit raises the batting average by 20 points (.020), and each out reduces it by the same amount. Using the result of entire games not only means that the running average may be kept from newspaper box scores but reduces the variability from one point to another. The use of even larger units (e.g., a series or a week) would reduce this variability even more.

Therefore, this player was somewhat more "streaky" than we would expect. There are fewer runs because his outs tend to come in a row rather than spread out. If the difference $(25.6 - 22 = 3.6)$ is divided by a factor that indicates the random variation expected, the standard deviation, it is possible to determine whether the obtained difference is likely to be a chance difference.

The divisor is

$$SD = SQRT \ (2 \times O \times B) \times (2 \times O \times B - O - B) / (B + O)^2 \times (B + O - 1)$$
$$SD = SQRT \ (2 \times 35 \times 19) \times (2 \times 35 \times 19 - 35 - 19) / (54^2 \times 53) = 3.3$$

And the ratio is

$$Z = (Runs - M) / SD = 3.6 / 3.3 = 1.09$$

Table 1 in Appendix C may be used to evaluate the ratio. Values of the ratio (Z) larger than values in the table will occur with the tabled frequency. For example, values larger than 1.09 will occur more than 25 percent of the time by chance. This player appears to reach base at random.

Conditional Probability

Conditional probability refers to the probability of some event depending upon (conditional upon) some other event. For example, the probability that a pitcher will be removed from the game is conditional upon the number of innings he has pitched.

Conditional probabilities may be used to evaluate sequences. If successive plate appearances are independent, then the probability of a hit following an out should be the same as the probability of a hit following another hit. If the player is streaky, his hits should come in bunches, and the probability of a hit following another hit should be greater than the probability of a hit following an out. Here is a sequence of hits and outs:

O O O H O O H O O H O O H O O O O H O O H O O H H O
O O H H

In this sequence of 30 at-bats, there are 10 hits. This string may be analyzed using a simple chi-square. The expected values are based on the fact that the overall probability of a hit is .33 and the probability of an out is .67. In the sequence there are 9 hits that were followed by another plate appearance. Seven of those 9 hits were followed by an out, and for the remaining 2 hits, the next plate appearance resulted in another hit. Based on

the probability of a hit, there should have been .33 × 9, or 3 hits following hits and .67 × 9 = 6 outs following hits. Observed and expected values following outs are determined in the same way. The chi-square is then computed in the usual way.

	Obs.	Exp.	O-E	Sq/E
Following hits (9):				
Hit	2	3	−1	.33
Out	7	6	1	.17
Following outs (20):				
Hit	8	6.6	1.4	.30
Out	12	13.4	−1.4	.15

Chi-square = .95

The low value of chi-square suggests that the sequence deviates from randomness only by chance.

Analysis by Game

Throughout this book we have concentrated on analysis of the individual plate appearance, at-bat, or batter faced. It is also possible to use the individual game as the basic unit. These analyses require only the use of box scores, which are readily available to most fans.

Means, Variances, and Standard Errors

Almost any statistic may be computed for a batter or pitcher for a single game. These statistics may then be treated as single values and averaged over a series of games. On the next page is a summary of 10 games played by Don Mattingly.

The advantage of this procedure is that it provides measures of the player's variability. The standard deviation indicates his day-to-day variability in performance, and the standard error provides an estimate of the variability of the mean for that number of games. For those measures that are pure proportions (batting average, on-base average), the standard error should be close to that estimated by SQRT $(BA \times (1 - BA)) / AB$.

It is important to note, however, that the mean value of the statistic, because it weights each day's performance equally regardless of the number

Date	AB	1B	2B	3B	HR	BB	BA	OB	SLG	BRUNS
5/22	4	2	1	0	0	1	.750	.800	1.000	1.77
5/23	3	0	0	0	0	0	.000	.000	.000	−.81
5/24	4	0	0	0	1	1	.250	.400	1.000	.96
5/25	5	1	1	0	1	0	.600	.600	1.400	2.12
5/26	3	0	0	0	1	2	.333	.600	1.333	1.25
5/27	5	1	0	0	0	0	.200	.200	.200	−.62
5/28	4	1	1	0	0	0	.500	.500	.750	.72
5/30	4	2	0	0	0	0	.500	.500	.500	.38
6/1	3	0	0	0	0	1	.000	.250	.000	−.48
6/3	5	1	1	0	0	0	.400	.400	.600	.45
Mean							.353	.425	.678	.574
SD							.246	.230	.511	.997
SE							.077	.073	.161	.315

of plate appearances, will not exactly equal the overall statistic. For example, the overall batting average for the above games was 15 / 40 = .375, and the mean was .353. With a large number of games, however, the discrepancy will be smaller. Since batting runs does not involve weighting the daily total by plate appearances, the sum of batting runs over games will be the same as the batting runs determined from the total number of plate appearances. This property makes game-by-game analysis particularly apt for batting runs.

Another particular advantage of averaging over games is that it makes it possible to obtain a measure of variability for nonadditive statistics (e.g., production index, runs created, total average, earned run average, etc.) that cannot be obtained from the analysis of overall plate appearances. This is particularly helpful since the production index and earned run average are easy to compute from individual game records. For nonadditive statistics, however, the mean over games may be quite different from the overall statistic, particularly when there is a multiplicative component in the numerator.

One application of the game-by-game analysis is the comparison of a player's performance in different sets of games. The analysis of variance procedure (Chapter 14) may be used with these measures to determine the significance of differences.

Example: Roger Clemens pitched in 33 games in the 1986 season, 16 at home and 17 on the road. Does he pitch better in one context than the other? Begin by computing the earned run average for *each* mound appearance:

Home Games			Road Games		
IP	ER	ERA	IP	ER	ERA
7	1	1.29	8.2	1	1.04
6.2	3	4.05	8.1	4	4.32
9	1	1.00	8	5	5.63
8	1	1.13	9	1	1.00
9	5	5.00	8	2	2.25
8	2	2.25	9	0	0.00
7.1	4	4.91	8	1	1.13
5	5	9.00	9	1	1.00
9	1	1.00	8	2	2.25
9	0	0.00	8	4	4.50
7.2	5	5.87	9	1	1.00
7	3	3.86	4.1	2	4.15
7	1	1.29	6	3	4.50
9	1	1.00	9	1	1.00
9	0	0.00	8	2	2.25
1.2	1	5.40	6	4	6.00
			8	2	2.25

Sums	47.05			44.27
Mean	2.94			2.60
SD	2.57			1.84
SE	.64			.45

The analysis of variance would proceed as follows:

$$SSt = 1.29^2 + 4.05^2 + \ldots 2.25^2 - 91.32^2 / 33 = 408.39 - 252.71 = 155.68$$
$$SSc = 47.05^2 / 16 + 44.27^2 / 17 - 252.71 = .93$$
$$SSe = 155.68 - .93 = 154.75$$

$$Var(c) = .93 / 1 = .93$$
$$Var(e) = 154.75 / 31 = 4.99$$

$$F = .93 / 4.99 = .19$$

Several things may be obtained from these kinds of analyses. First there is the conclusion with respect to the difference between conditions. In this case, since F is less than 1.00, the difference between home and road performance is likely to be a chance difference. More important, however, it provides an indication of the game-by-game variability in Clemens's performance in terms of the standard error. The overall standard error for his earned run average that season was .39. This standard error may be interpreted like any other standard error. One may use it to estimate confidence intervals or to predict the potential range of values for future seasons, just as we have done previously for other statistics.

Multiple-Hit Games

Another analysis that may be of interest is the distribution of hits over games. A batter who has a .250 batting average will average 1 hit every 4 at-bats, but his game-by-game performance will be highly variable— sometimes going hitless, sometimes getting multiple hits. Data obtainable from box scores enables us to describe just how a batter's hits are distributed over games. Here are some data from Alvin Davis's record in 146 games. The columns represent the number of hits in a game, and the rows represent the number of at-bats in a game. The entries are the number of games in which h hits were obtained in b at-bats. For example, the third row features games with 4 at-bats. There were 68 such games (listed in the totals column). Davis had 20 hitless games, 25 games with 1 hit, 18 games with 2 hits, and so on. Therefore, the column totals represent the number of games in which he had 0, 1, 2 hits, regardless of the number of at-bats.

	Hits					
At-Bats	0	1	2	3	4	Tot
6	0	0	4	1	1	6
5	4	12	13	5	0	34
4	20	25	18	5	0	68
3	12	5	4	0	–	21
2	3	1	1	–	–	5
1	9	3	–	–	–	12
Totals	48	46	40	11	1	146

These frequencies may be treated like any other frequency statistic. They may be converted to proportions (the proportions are proportions of games, not plate appearances or at-bats) to compare players with different frequencies in the total column. The same kind of data may be compiled for pitchers. For example, the columns might represent innings pitched; the rows, hits allowed.

There are various uses for distributions of this type. They may be compared with those expected if the distribution of hits over plate appearances or at-bats is random. This involves computing the expected value for each entry in the table. This is a rather tedious procedure, although it is fairly simple. For any given number of at-bats, y, the first step is to compute the probability of x, hits. This is done in two steps. First,

$$P = (BA)^x \times (1 - BA)^{y-x}$$

In the above table, the overall batting average is $163 / 563 = .290$. Therefore, the probability of 1 hit given 4 at-bats (a conditional probability) is

$$P = (.290)^1 \times (1 - .289)^{4-1} = .104$$

This is actually an application of the joint rule from Chapter 16. The probability of 1 hit in 4 at-bats is equal to the joint probability of 1 hit and 3 outs (the product of the individual probabilities). This is the probability of *any* sequence of 1 hit and 4 outs. The batter, however, may go 1 for 4 in four ways; his lone hit could occur on any of the 4 at-bats.

Therefore, applying the either-or rule, the probability of 4 hits occurring is the sum of the probabilities for each of the four possible combinations.

$$P \text{ (1 for 4)} = 4 \times .104 = .416$$

This is the conditional probability of 1 hit given 4 at-bats. From the last column, we see that there were 68 games in which the player had 4 at-bats. He should therefore have 1 hit in 4 at-bats in .416 of those games. The expected number of 1-for-4 games $= .416 \times 68 = 28.3$. The actual number of 1-for-4 games (25) is somewhat less than expected.

Computations for each of the other entries in the table are carried out in a similar manner. Computation of the P values are straightforward. The number of different ways a player may get x hits in y at-bats may be computed using a formula for combinations, but since few at-bats are involved in any game, here is a table of the necessary values for up to 6 at-bats.

			Hits				
At-Bats	0	1	2	3	4	5	6
1	1	1					
2	1	2	1				
3	1	3	3	1			
4	1	4	6	4	1		
5	1	5	10	10	5	1	
6	1	6	15	20	15	6	1

For example, the third entry in the third row says that there are three possible combinations of 1 hit and 2 outs. Therefore,

$$P(1 \text{ for } 3) = 3 \times (BA)^1 \times (1 - BA)^{3-1}$$

When all of the expected frequencies have been obtained, the difference between observed and expected values may be tested for significance using chi-square. If some of the expected values are too small (less than 5), some of the entries may be combined, or the test may be carried out on the column totals. In computing the chi-square, be sure to use all of the cells for which an expected value is possible, even if there are no entries (e.g., 6 for 6). A significant chi-square in this analysis indicates that the distribution of hits over games is not random. For example, a player might have more "0-fers" and multiple-hit games and fewer single-hit games than expected.

Fielding and Pitching: A Parting Shot

We have previously pointed out the two major problems with analyzing baseball defense: (1) the inevitable confounding of pitching and fielding; and (2) the confoundings inherent in the definition of a fielding chance. Clearly, data from pitching and fielding lines are inadequate to permit an unbiased index of pitching or fielding contributions of individual players.

Fielding

Recent innovations in scoring, however, may make it possible to evaluate fielding objectively and to separate its contribution from pitching. The necessary requirement, a definition of *fielding chance* that is independent of the fielder's behavior, has recently appeared in some published summaries.* Essentially, it requires recording data that heretofore has resided only in the intuitions of fans, managers, players, and media.

For each fielding position, a *zone* is circumscribed in which balls are deemed playable. For example, a shortstop's zone is described as 25 feet in each direction from the "normal" position. A player's *zone rating* is the proportion of balls in the zone that result in outs plus outs obtained on balls outside the zone.

This eliminates a number of important biases in fielding statistics, most notably ground ball–fly-ball bias in pitching or chance factors related to where balls are hit. The published values given are not quite true proportions because players are given extra credit for fielding balls outside the zone and are credited with two outs for a double play. Nor is it a complete

---

*The Stats Baseball Scoreboard, *published by Stats Inc., contains some of this fielding data, and more complete numbers are available on special order. They are able to provide these data because they score every major league game according to the recording system they have devised. The data are not included in the official records.*

measure since pop flies and other "air balls" are not included. This means that performance on a per-ground-ball basis cannot be ascertained since the errors and double play totals in baseball guides include line drives, pop flies, and other types.

Clearly, this is one case where the reliability of the scorer will be put to a severe test. Judgments of when a ball is within the zone may prove highly variable from scorer to scorer since there are no lines on the field to tell him when a ball was inside the zone. The scorer may also be subject to biases produced by preconceptions of a player's fielding ability or his gracefulness or style.

For outfielders, two values are necessary. One is a zone rating similar to that of infielders. The second is the *cannon factor*. The problem with outfield assists has always been that runners who respect an outfielder's arm will not go for the extra base, thus depriving the fielder of a chance for an assist. The cannon factor assigns a *base taken* whenever a runner advances two bases on a single, three on a double, when the hit is in his zone. Otherwise, he gets a *hold*. The number of extra bases divided by the total of the two provides a proportional index of the effectiveness of the outfielder in preventing advancement. Again, the reliability of the scorer's judgment may be put to a severe test.

Pitching

Although pitching and fielding are totally confounded in the pitching and fielding lines, the zone data may also be valuable in separating the two components. If fielders can be given a zone rating, so can pitchers. For example, it should be possible to compute the proportion of batters that hit balls within the zones, within a particular zone, or a graded set of zones, thus creating a *catchable ball index* for the pitcher. This would more equitably assess the pitcher who is cursed by an infield or outfield of slugs or blessed with great support.

Appendix A:
Category Abbreviations

A	Assist (fielder)
AB	At-bat: plate appearance minus the number of bases on balls, hit by pitcher, sacrifices, and sacrifice flies
BB	Bases on balls
BF or BFP	Batters faced by pitcher
CG	Complete game by pitcher
CS	Caught stealing
DP	Participates in double plays (fielder)
E	Error
ER	Earned runs
G	Games played
GF	Games finished by relief pitcher
GIDP	Grounded into double plays
GR *GS*	Games relieved *Games Started*
H	Total hits, the sum of singles, doubles, triples, and home runs
HB	Hit batters
HP	Hit by pitcher
HR	Home runs
IBB or Int.BB	Intentional bases on balls
IG	Games started but not completed by pitcher
IP	Innings pitched
L	Games lost by pitcher
ND	Games pitched with no decision
NR	Plate appearances in which run was not scored
OH	Other hits: total hits minus home runs
PA	Plate appearances; this is usually the number of times a player comes to bat but may exclude sacrifice bunts
PO	Putouts (fielder)
R	Runs scored
RBI	Runs batted in
SB	Stolen bases

SF	Sacrifice flies (fly-ball outs scoring a runner)
SH	Sacrifice bunts
ShO	Shutouts
SO	Strikeouts
Sv	Save
TB	Total bases: $(1B \times 1) + (2B \times 2) + (3B \times 3) + (HR \times 4)$
TBF	Batters faced by pitcher
TC	Total fielding chances
UR	Unearned runs
W	Games won by pitcher
WP	Wild pitches
1B	Singles
2B	Doubles
3B	Triples

Appendix B:
Reliability, Sums and Squares

I. Reliability of the Slugging
Average: Computational Example

	Boggs	Henderson	Bell	Clark	Ripken	Total
AB	584	507	614	496	512	2713
TB	286	266	274	215	132	1173
1	2	0	4	0	0	
2	0	0	0	0	1	
3	0	1	1	0	0	
4	1	1	0	4	0	
•	•	•	•	•	•	
•	•	•	•	•	•	
a. Sum	286	266	274	215	132	1173
b. Squares	472	365	646	567	198	2248

The sum is simply the sum of total bases. The squares must be calculated from the singles, doubles, triples, and home runs. Simply multiply the *square* of the bases gained on that hit times their number. For example, Boggs had 158 singles, 45 doubles, 6 triples, and 5 home runs. Therefore, the squares for Boggs would be $(158 \times 1) + (45 \times 4) + (6 \times 9) + (5 \times 16) = 472$.

The calculation of R then proceeds as indicated in Chapter 7:

Corrector $(C) = 1173^2 / 2713 = 507.16$
SS $(Tot) = (2248 - 507.16) = 1740.84$
SS $(Players) = 286^2 / 584 + 266^2 / 507 \ldots + 132^2 / 512 - 507.16 =$
$140.06 + 139.56 + 122.27 + 93.20 + 34.03 - 507.16 = 21.96$
SS $(error\ within) = 1740.84 - 21.96 = 1718.88$

Variances:

> Var(X) = 21.96 / No. of Players minus 1 = 21.96 / 4 = 5.49
> Var(E) = 1718.88 / Total AB − No. of Players = 2713 − 5 = 1718.88 / 2708 = .635
> R = 1 − .634 / 5.49 = 1 − .116 = .884

II. Calculation of Sums and Squares for Total Offense and Batting Runs

---

When the results of attempted steals are included in total offense or batting runs, it complicates the calculation of R. Simply adding or subtracting the (weighted) values for successes and failures from the sum of bases gained or weighted bases gained will produce neither an accurate sum (row a in the table) nor an accurate value for squares (row b). Since the bases gained *on each plate appearance* must be summed and squared, we do not know which events preceded a steal or being caught, so we do not know the individual values. If a player reaches first base on a single or walk, a steal "converts" a value of 1 into a value of 2. If he reached on a fielder's choice or error, it converts a 0 into a 1. If he is caught stealing, it converts a 1 into a 0 or a 0 into a −1. Steals of third provide even more problems, and attempts at third are normally not differentiated from those at second.

We have pointed out before that stolen bases are infrequent enough that they have little effect on measures of total offense, except for a few players. If the number of players in the list being examined is large, distortions in the totals for these players will have little effect.

Second, it is sound practice to use some procedure that will underestimate the value of R. You will then know that the true reliability cannot be any lower than the value obtained. Since the sum of bases gained for each player, hence Var(X), is unaffected by any of the above problems, the best solution is to assign stolen-base data to maximize the squares, hence Var(E). This will occur if every steal is assumed to follow a hit. Here is an example for Tim Raines in 1989.

PA	1B	2B	3B	HR	BB	Outs	SB	CS
618	104	29	6	9	96	374	41	8

If stolen-base data for third base are available, the values for the sum (a) and squares (b) are computed by assuming that all steals of second follow singles and that all steals of third follow doubles. Therefore, every attempted steal of second subtracts from singles. If it is successful, it adds to doubles; if not, it adds to outs. Likewise, every attempt at third subtracts from doubles. If it is successful, it adds to triples; if not, it adds to outs (essentially giving it a value of −2).

Of Raines's 49 attempts, 39 of them were at second base, of which 32 were successful. Of the remaining 10, which were at third, he was successful on 9. The revised totals for Raines would therefore be

PA 1B 2B 3B HR BB Outs
618 65 51 15 9 96 382

Singles = 104 – 39 attempts = 65
Doubles = 29 + 32 successes at second – 10 attempts at third = 51
Triples = 6 + 9 successes = 15
Outs = 374 + 7 outs at second + 1 out at third = 382

The necessary quantities for Raines would then be

a. sum = $65 + (2 \times 51) + (3 \times 15) + (4 \times 9) + 96 = 344$
b. squares = $65 + (4 \times 51) + (9 \times 15) + (16 \times 9) + 96 = 644$

If data on steals of third are not known, they may be taken as 25 percent of the attempts. The success rate is normally somewhat higher for third, but not dramatically so. It would not distort the data much to use the same success rate for each base.

With respect to batting runs, the situation is somewhat more complex. In fact, it is not clear whether the computation of R should even be attempted with batting runs. Technically, the run value of a single followed by a successful or unsuccessful steal probably does not have the same run potential as the sum of those events. Since steals add little to batting runs for most players, it is probably best to compute R for batting runs without these data.

The computation for Raines:

a. (sum) = $(.46 \times 104) + (.8 \times 29) + (1.02 \times 6) + (1.4 \times 9) + (.33 \times 96) - (.25 \times 382) = 25.9$
b. (squares) = $(.46^2 \times 104) + (.8^2 \times 29) + (1.02^2 \times 6) + (1.4^2 \times 9) + (.33^2 \times 96) -$
$(.25^2 \times 382) = 51.02$

Appendix C: Value Tables

Table 1. Percentage Values for Z

Z	Pct.	Z	Pct.	Z	Pct.
3.30	.001	1.64	.10	−1.44	.85
2.81	.005	1.44	.15	−1.64	.90
2.58	.01	1.15	.25	−1.96	.95
2.32	.02	0	.50	−2.58	.98
1.96	.05	−1.15	.75	−2.81	.99

Table 2. Criterion Values for Chi-square

d.f.	.20	.10	.05	.01
1	1.64	2.71	3.84	6.64
2	3.22	4.60	5.99	9.21
3	4.64	6.25	7.82	11.34
4	5.99	7.78	9.49	13.28
5	7.29	9.24	11.07	15.09
6	8.56	10.64	12.59	16.81
7	9.80	12.02	14.07	18.48
8	11.03	13.36	15.51	20.09
9	13.44	15.99	16.92	21.67

Table 3. Criterion Values for *F* for 5%

Denom df	Numerator df			
	1	2	3	4[a]
4	7.71	6.94	6.59	6.39
8	5.32	4.46	4.07	3.84
10	4.96	4.10	3.71	3.48
12	4.75	3.88	3.49	3.26
16	4.49	3.63	3.24	3.01
20	4.35	3.49	3.10	2.87
30	4.17	3.32	2.92	2.69
60	4.00	3.15	2.76	2.53
100	3.94	3.09	2.70	2.46
200	3.89	3.04	2.65	2.41
400	3.86	3.02	2.62	2.39
1000	3.85	3.00	2.61	2.38
inf	3.84	2.99	2.60	2.37

[a]More extensive tables for *F* are available in most introductory textbooks on statistical analysis.

Appendix D: Computation Examples, Variance

---

1. Chi-square Three-Way Classification

Boggs's Batting Average for Successive Thirds of the Season		Obt	Expect	O-E	Squared	/ Exp
Apr–May	Hits	52	58.74	−6.74	45.43	.773
	Outs	126	119.26	6.74	45.43	.381
June–July	Hits	73	66.00	7.00	49.00	.742
	Outs	127	134.00	−7.00	49.00	.366
Aug–Sept	Hits	80	80.19	−.19	.04	.0005
	Outs	163	162.81	.19	.04	.0002
Chi-square						2.26

---

2. Analysis of Variance Computation Examples

Warning: The results of these analyses are not to be taken seriously. The players for each analysis were chosen for computational convenience rather than representativeness.

178

A. More Than Two Conditions

Case I: Separate Groups

Earned Run Average:
Three Types of Pitchers

Strikeout Pitchers		Fly-Ball Pitchers		Ground-Ball Pitchers	
Ryan	3.20	Stewart	3.22	Dopson	3.99
Saberhagen	2.16	Swindell	3.37	Gubicza	3.04
Clemens	3.13	Alexander	4.44	Hough	4.35
Bosio	2.95	Bankhead	3.34	Brown	3.35
Moore	2.61	Hawkins	4.80	Abbott	3.92
Sum	14.05		19.17		18.65
Squares	40.2171		75.6345		70.6731

Total Sum = 51.87
Total Squares = 186.5247

$C = 51.87^2 / 15 = 179.3665$

$SStot = 186.5247 - 179.3665 = 7.16$
$SScond = (14.05^2 + 19.17^2 + 18.65^2) / 5 - 179.3665 = 3.18$
$SSwithin\ c = 7.16 - 3.18 = 3.98$

$Var(C) = 3.18 / 2 = 1.59$
$Var(P.c) = 3.98 / 12 = .332$

$1.59 / .332 = 4.79$
The critical value of F is found in row 4, column 2, of Table 3 (3.88).

Case II: Within Players

	Apr–May	June–July	Aug–Sept	Total
	Production Index for Successive Thirds of Season			
Johnson	858	1083	825	2766[a]
Davis	938	961	853	2752
Ripken	741	735	687	2163
McGriff	956	913	904	2773
Henderson	801	872	764	2437
Sums	4294	4564	4033	12,891
Squares	3,720,626	4,230,588	3,281,115	33,531,327

[a]PI is not additive. Nevertheless, this column is the unweighted sum of the three components, not the overall PI. Decimals have been omitted.

$C = 12,891^2 / 15 = 11,078,525.4$

$SStot = 858^2 + 938^2 \ldots + 764^2 - 11,078,525.4 = 153,803.6$
$SScond = (4294^2 + 4564^2 + 4033^2) / 5 - 11,078,525.4 = 28,198.6$
$SSplayers = (2766^2 + \ldots 2437^2) / 3 - 11,078,525.4 = 98,583.6$
$SSint = 153,803.6 - 28,198.6 - 98,583.6 = 27,021.4$

$Var(cond) = 28,198.6 / 2 = 14,099.3$
$Var(int) = 27,021.4 / 8 = 3,377.75$

$F = 4.17$

The critical value of F is found in row 2, column 2, of Table 3 (4.46).

Case III: Separate Groups

On-base Average vs. Three Types of Pitchers

Strikeout Pitchers			Fly-Ball Pitchers			Ground-Ball Pitchers		
	BF	OB		BF	OB		BF	OB
Ryan	979	269	Stewart	1072	335	Dopson	722	237
Saberhagen	1012	254	Swindell	745	221	Gubicza	1049	320
Clemens	1035	316	Alexander	968	326	Hough	792	269
Bosio	964	279	Bankhead	858	253	Brown	795	241
Moore	971	278	Hawkins	905	320	Abbott	777	268
Sum	4961	1396		4548	1455		4135	1335

$C = (1396 + 1455 + 1335)^2 / (4961 + 4548 + 4135) = 1284.27$

$SScond = (1396^2 / 4961) + (1455^2 / 4548) + (1335^2 / 4135) - 1284.27 = 5.05$

$SSPw1 = (269^2 / 979) + \ldots (278^2 / 971) - (1396^2 / 4961) = 1.65$

$SSPw2 = (335^2 / 1072) + \ldots + (320^2 / 905) - (1455^2 / 4548) = 2.30$

$SSPw3 = (237^2 / 722) + \ldots + (268^2 / 777) - (1335^2 / 4135) = 1.28$

$Var(C) = 5.05 / 2 = 2.53$

$Var(Pwc) = (1.65 + 2.30 + 1.28) / 12 = .44$

$F = 2.53 / .44 = 5.75$

The critical value of F is found in row 4, column 2, of Table 3 (3.88).

Case IV: Within Players

Batting Average for Successive Thirds of Season

	Apr–May		June–July		Aug–Sept		Total	
	AB	H	AB	H	AB	H	AB	H
Johnson	162	42	195	62	111	57	468	161
Davis	143	48	155	52	197	51	495	151
Ripken	193	56	229	59	222	51	644	166
McGriff	179	53	187	48	181	46	547	147
Henderson	184	50	169	51	186	47	539	148
Sums	861	249	935	272	897	252	2693	773

$C = 773^2 / 2693 = 221.88$

$SStot = (42^2 / 162) + (48^2 / 143) + \ldots (47^2 / 186) - 221.88 = 8.49$
$SScond = (249^2 / 861) + (272^2 / 935) + (252^2 / 897) - 221.94 - 221.88 = .06$
$SSplayers = (161^2 / 468) + \ldots (148^2 / 539) - 223.93 - 221.88 = 2.05$
$SSint = 8.49 - .06 - 2.05 = 6.38$

$Var(cond) = .06 / 2 = .03$
$Var(int) = 6.38 / 8 = .80$

$F = .03 / .80$ (F is less than 1.00)
The critical value of F is found in row 2, column 2, Table 3 (4.46).

B. *The Factorial Design*

This arrangement allows for the simultaneous evaluation of two factors plus their interaction. The example is for a 2×2 factorial.

Case I: Separate Groups

Production Index for Left- and Right-Handed
Ground-Ball or Fly-Ball Hitters

LH-GB		RH-GB		LH-FB		RH-FB	
Butler	785	Fermin	604	Nokes	680	Bell	730
Gwynn	778	Pena	672	Clark	812	Williams	809
Johnson	684	Puckett	813	Joyner	749	Sabo	821
Thompson	620	Sax	644	Mattingly	651	Wallach	814
Harris	723	Quintana	738	Strawberry	882	Fielder	972
Sums	3590		3471		3774		4146
Squares	2,596,494		2,436,749		2,884,470		3,468,802

Totals: 14,981   Squares = 11,386,515

Left-handed = 7364   Right-handed = 7617

Ground Ball = 7061   Fly Ball = 7920

$C = 14,981^2 / 20 = 11,221,518.05$

$SStot = 11,386,515 - 11,221,518.05 = 164,996.95$
$SScond = (3590^2 + \ldots + 4146^2) / 5 - 11,221,518.05 = 52,147.95$
$SSlh\text{-}rh = (7364^2 + 7617^2) / 10 - 11,221,518.05 = 3200.45$
$SSgb\text{-}fb = (7061^2 + 7920^2) / 10 - 11,221,518.05 = 36,894.05$
$SSint = 52,147.95 - 3,200.45 - 36,894.05 = 12,053.45$
$SSpwc = 164,996.95 - 52,147.95 = 112,849$

$Var(lh\text{-}rh) = 3200.45 / 1 = 3200.45$
$Var(gb\text{-}fb) = 36,894.05 / 1 = 36,894.05$
$Var(int) = 12,053.45 / 1 = 12,053.45$
$Var(pwc) = 112,849 / 16 = 7053.06$

$F(lh\text{-}rh) = 3,200.45 / 7053.06 = 454$ (*F* is less than 1)
$F(gb\text{-}fb) = 36,894.05 / 7053.06 = 5.23$
$F(int) = 12,053.45 / 7053.06 = 1.71$

The critical value for all three *F*'s is obtained from row 5, column 1, Table 3
(4.49). The difference between ground- and fly-ball hitters is significant. Neither
handedness nor the interaction had an effect.

Case II: One Factor Is Within Players

Earned Run Average for Ground-Ball and Fly-Ball Pitchers
on Turf and Grass (Road Games Only, 1986)

Ground Ball	Grass	Turf	Total	Fly Ball	Grass	Turf	Total
Clemens	2.49	2.20	4.69	Browning	3.50	4.40	7.90
Correa	4.11	4.93	9.04	Clancy	2.93	4.86	7.79
Forsch	3.57	4.40	7.97	Darling	3.89	2.91	6.80
Hershiser	4.30	5.25	9.55	Gullicksen	3.98	1.69	5.67
Knepper	2.72	2.45	5.17	Niekro	5.24	3.03	8.27
Sums	17.19	19.23	36.42		19.54	16.89	36.43
Squares	61.7255	82.0699	285.1700		79.2650	63.4847	269.8759

Total = 72.85

Squares = 286.5451

$C = 72.85^2 / 20 = 265.36$

$SStot = 286.5451 - 265.36 = 21.19$

$SScond = (17.19^2 + \ldots 16.89^2) / 5 - 265.36 = 1.11$

$SSgb\text{-}fb = (36.42^2 + 36.43^2) / 10 - 265.36 = 0.00$

$SStgr\text{-}t = ((17.19 + 19.54)^2 + (19.23 + 16.89)^2) / 10 - 265.36 = .01$

$SSint \ (cond) = 1.11 - .01 = 1.10$

$SSplayers = (285.1700 + 269.8759) / 2 - 265.36 = 12.16$

$SSpwc = 12.16 - 0 = 12.16$

$SSint. \ players = 21.19 - 12.16 - .01 - 1.10 = 7.92$

Var(gb-fb) = 0

Var(gr-t) = .01 / 1 = .01

Var(int-cond) = 1.10 / 1 = 1.10

Var(pwc) = 12.16 / 8 = 1.52

Var(int-players) = 7.92 / 8 = .99

This procedure is different because the denominator for F depends upon whether the factor is a separate-groups factor (ground ball vs. fly ball) or a within-players factor (grass vs. turf). For separate groups, the denominator is the Var(p.c.) based on SSp.c. of 12.16, divided by the number of players −1, minus the number of conditions, minus 1 $(10 - 1) - (2 - 1) = 8$. For any factor that involves a within-players component (in this case that is both grass-turf and the interaction between conditions), the denominator is Var(int-players), which is based on SSint.players. The SS is obtained by subtracting SSplayers from SStot, then subtracting the SS for each of the within-players factors from the remainder. Var(int.players) is then obtained by dividing the SS by the number of values used in the analysis (20) minus (1+ the sum of all of the other denominators).

F(gb-fb) = Var(gb-fb) / Var(int-players) is less than 1.00
F(gr-t) = Var(gr-t) / Var(int-players) = .01 / .99 is less than 1.00
F(int-cond) = Var(int-cond) / Var(int-players) = 1.10 / .99 = 1.11

The critical values of F are obtained from row 2, column 1, Table 3 (5.32). None of the factors in this analysis had a significant effect, despite the apparent "crossover" interaction.

Road games only were used, so that an effect of home vs. road games would not be confused with turf-grass differences that result from the type of playing surface for home games.

Case III: Separate Groups

Slugging Average for Left- and Right-handed
Ground-Ball and Fly-Ball Hitters

LH-GB	AB	TB	RH-GB	AB	TB
Butler	622	239	Fermin	414	126
Gwynn	573	238	Pena	491	171
Johnson	541	193	Puckett	551	246
Thompson	418	136	Sax	615	200
Harris	431	161	Quintana	512	196
Sums	2585	967		2583	939

LH-FB	AB	TB	RH-FB	AB	TB
Nokes	351	131	Bell	562	237
Clark	600	269	Williams	617	301
Joyner	310	122	Sabo	567	270
Mattingly	394	132	Wallach	626	295
Strawberry	542	281	Fielder	573	339
Sums	2197	935		2945	1442

Totals:	AB	TB
Left-handed	4782	1902
Right-handed	5528	2381
Ground Ball	5168	1906
Fly Ball	5142	2377
Overall	10,310	4283

$C = 4283^2 / 10,310 = 1779.25$

$SStot = 239^2 / 622 + 238^2 / 573 + \ldots 339^2 / 573 - C = 54.83$
$SScond = 967^2 / 2585 + \ldots 1442^2 / 2945 - C = 27.84$
$SSlh\text{-}rh = 1902^2 / 4782 + 2381^2 / 5528 - C = 2.79$
$SSgb\text{-}fb = 1906^2 / 5168 + 2377^2 / 5142 - C = 22.52$
$SSint = 27.84 - 2.79 - 22.52 = 2.53$
$SSpwc = 54.83 - 27.84 = 26.99$

$Var(lh\text{-}rh) = 2.79 / 1 = 2.79$
$Var(gb\text{-}fb) = 22.52 / 1 = 22.52$
$Var(int) = 2.53 / (1 \times 1) = 2.53$
$Var(pwc) = 27.01 / (20 - 4) = 1.69$

$F(lh\text{-}rh) = 2.79 / 1.69 = 1.65$
$F(gb\text{-}fb) = 22.52 / 1.69 = 13.33$
$F(int) = 2.53 / 1.69 = 1.50$

The critical value of F is obtained from column 1, row 5, Table 3 (4.49). Therefore, fly-ball hitters have a significantly higher slugging average than ground-ball hitters ($F = 13.33$). Batting handedness does not have an overall effect, however ($F = 1.65$), nor is there any interaction ($F = 1.50$) despite the fact that the difference is larger for right-handers.

Index